God Says I AM

A Guide to Fruitful
Affirmations and Declarations

(Learn to BE, AGREE, and DECREE)

Otescia R. Johnson

Scripture quotations marked (NKJV) are taken from the New King James Version®. Copyright © 1982 by Thomas Nelson. Used by permission. All rights reserved.

Scripture quotations marked (NLT) are taken from the Holy Bible, New Living Translation, copyright ©1996, 2004, 2015 by Tyndale House Foundation. Used by permission of Tyndale House Publishers, Carol Stream, Illinois 60188. All rights reserved.

Scripture quotations marked (AMP) are taken from the Amplified Bible, Copyright © 1954, 1958, 1962, 1964, 1965, 1987 by The Lockman Foundation. Used by permission.

GOD SAYS I AM- A Guide to Fruitful Affirmations and Declarations.

Copyright © 2021 All rights reserved — Otescia R. Johnson

No part of this publication may be reproduced or transmitted in any form or by any means, graphic, electronic, or mechanical, including photocopying, recording, taping, or by an information storage retrieval system without the written permission of the publisher. The only exception is brief quotations in printed reviews.

Please direct all copyright inquiries to:
B.O.Y. Enterprises, Inc.
c/o Author Copyrights
P.O. Box 1012
Lowell, NC 28098

Paperback ISBN: 978-1-955605-16-8

Cover and Interior Design: B.O.Y. Enterprises, Inc.

Printed in the United States.

Dedication
To the forerunners and world changers who are discovering the authority and power of their own voice.

Other books by Otescia R. Johnson

He Cheated: A Woman's Guide to Receiving God's Healing After Adultery

Lessons I Learned in the Divorce

I Am Who I Am… and I'm Finally Cool with Her

He Cheated: 2nd Edition

Goodbye Egypt: A Kingdom Entrepreneur's Guide to Reclaiming the Marketplace

Behold… I Give You Power Success Planner

Merging Faith and Business Planner

Otescia's books are available on all major book retailer websites.

Table of Contents

Preface 9

Introduction 13

Chapter 1 23
   I Am an Atmosphere Shifter

Chapter 2 33
   I Am Accepted

Chapter 3 47
   I Am Wealthy

Chapter 4 57
   I am a Prayer Warrior

Chapter 5 75
   I am a Profitable Kingdom Entrepreneur

Chapter 6 87
   I am God's Beloved Daughter

Chapter 7 99
   I am a Champion

Chapter 8 109
   I am a Forerunner

Special Note from the Author 119

Daily Affirmations 120

About the Author 123

Preface

I've lost count of the number of iterations this book has gone through. I originally began with an intention to create a hybrid, a cross between an instructional book and a guided journal. I believed Holy Spirit was leading me to teach people how to properly write effective affirmation statements and declarations. In a way, this is still true. However, the intent of this book goes much deeper. As with all things God-inspired, I had to spend more time with Him to receive the full revelation.

A few years ago, I penned a book titled, *I Am Who I Am… and I'm Finally Cool with Her*. This book was a very transparent look at my personal journey of self-discovery and growth. I believed it to be one of my best pieces of nonfiction. It even debuted at #1 on Amazon in several categories and garnered local media attention. I was thrilled, but like most career writers, I quickly turned my thoughts to the next book… the next message God ordained to be released in the Earth. Though I was unaware, God knew that message held more meat. So, as I began penning this book, several people started messaging me about *I Am Who I Am… and I'm Finally Cool with Her*. People were reading the book for the first time and were sharing how much it was blessing them. I thought, wow God, you're breathing new life into that message. How cool! Literally… those were my thoughts as I attempted to move forward with the book you're currently reading.

Then one day, seemingly out of the blue, God began speaking to me regarding the connection between the two books. He showed me how He'd been revealing the puzzle pieces to me the whole time, but I missed them. (I'm the daughter who needs Him to make it ALL THE WAY CLEAR. I often miss the hints.)

The titles of the books should have been a clue, but that slipped right over my head. Then, the nudge to include the other book's title on the cover of this one slipped by me. Plus… this book's dedication was already written and points to the divine purpose of both books. Yeah… I know, I should have caught all that, but I didn't. I never set out to write books in a series format. I just write whatever I'm inspired to write at the time and Holy Spirit takes it from there. That's His job, to guide me in God's perfect will. My job is simply to be obedient to His instructions.

Now that we have gotten that out of the way, let me tell you a little about the book you are about to read. This book is not a fluffy feel-good message. It is a challenge, a call-to-action of sorts, designed to help you grow into the person you are designed to BE!

Through these pages, I will take you, the reader, along with me as I recall my journey from "I am FINALLY cool with who I am," to "Now how the heck am I supposed to BE who God called me to BE?" Getting to know myself and becoming comfortable with my quirks, eccentricities, naturally bourgeois nature, ridiculous silliness, love of random history facts, and general dislike of any and all injustice was just the starting point. Knowing the natural me is great, but I had to learn how to BE me... the real me, the me God saw before the creation of time, the one He knew before He formed me in my mother's belly. That ME is:

A Powerful Atmosphere Shifter
Accepted
Wealthy
A Prayer Warrior
A Profitable Entrepreneur
God's Beloved Daughter
A Champion
A Forerunner

If you notice, the list above does not describe my character traits as much of my first book in this series did. This list describes who I AM in God and in the Earth. These are not things I must work to become. I AM all of these things. I do not need permission to be me. I do not need to double check my heart to make sure I am not being arrogant because I didn't call myself these things... God created me with these identities INSIDE me. My outer shell simply houses the true essence of the woman God created to exist and maneuver in the Earth.

When you learn to operate from who you are as opposed to who you want to become, you tap into the power of agreement with Heaven. Through the pages of this book, I will endeavor to share with you how I learned to BE who I AM, how I verbally came into agreement with who I AM, and how I used legal decrees to command the Earth to come into agreement with who I AM.

Affirmations and declarations have been highjacked by the world's system long enough. Now, it is time for the children of God to learn how to use this Heavenly system to advance and promote the Kingdom of God in the Earth!

Introduction

Before we dive into the meat of this book, we must lay some groundwork. Often, the Believer does not see fruit from his/her efforts because we do not have full revelation of what we are doing. When this happens, it can leave one feeling frustrated and lead to abandonment of the practice. This is what has happened with affirmations and declarations. Because we do not understand how to accurately exercise the power of our tongues, we have accepted a lifestyle that is beneath where God has called us to live.

Let's begin by simply defining the words affirmation and declaration for the purposes of this book. We will look at the secular definition cited from Merriam-Webster's online dictionary as well as the biblical definitions cited from Strong's Complete Dictionary of Bible Words.

Affirmation comes from the root word affirm.

Merriam-Webster's Definition:

Affirm- 1a: validate, confirm **b:** to state positively
2: to assert (something, such as a judgment or decree) as valid or confirmed
3: to show or express a strong belief in or dedication to

Declaration- 1: the act of declaring: Announcement

2b: a statement made by a party to a legal transaction usually not under oath
3a: something that is <u>declared</u> a *declaration* of love
b: a document containing such a declaration

Strong's Definition:
Affirm- to confirm thoroughly
Declaration- utterance; recital, written account

When you form an affirmation, you are literally validating, thoroughly confirming, positively stating, asserting, and expressing a strong belief in or dedication to what you believe. This is why I AM statements are so important. Personal affirmations are "I AM" statements that express what you believe to be true about yourself. Effective I AM statements take it a step further. I will share more on this in a moment.

Declarations are the utterance, the legal statements, recitals, and written accounts of what you believe. In the natural, declarations are made during legal transactions. The same is true in the Spirit realm. When you make a declaration in alignment with the word of God, you release legislation that must be executed and/or carried out in the Spirit realm and manifested in the Earth.

One thing we must note about the Spirit realm is, for one to accomplish anything, FAITH must be present. Just as you use money to buy things in the Earth, you use faith to accomplish and obtain things in the Spirit. You wouldn't walk into your favorite store and expect to buy everything

Introduction

you want without having the money to pay for it. The same is true for the Kingdom of Heaven. There must be faith to "pay" for the things you desire.

This is why many Believers do not see the fruit of their affirmations and declarations. They release declarations without the knowledge, understanding, or even the faith to sustain their legislation. They state affirming statements, but again lack the faith to see their manifestation.

Manifestation Works Through Faith

The Bible teaches us in Romans 10:17 (NKJV) that faith comes by hearing, and hearing by the word of God. To have faith that you are who God says you are, you must HEAR the word of God. How will you hear the word of God spoken over *you* concerning *you*? You must repeat aloud what God has spoken to you during your personal quiet time with Him. When you ask Him to tell you who you are, He will do exactly that. Then, you turn what you heard into affirmation statements! The more you speak aloud what you've heard, the stronger your faith will become to believe what you've heard from Heaven and spoken aloud.

Am I saying the only reason a person does not see manifestation is because they lack faith? Of course not! Faith is the foundational thing. It is the currency. You must believe what you are saying and decreeing, but you must also be in alignment with the will of God. When you write or recite an I AM statement, you speak directly to your true identity in Christ. Effective I AM statements simply affirm what God has already said about you.

The Earth is Voice Activated

When God releases a word about you or anything concerning you, it is immediately established in Heaven. Time does not exist in Heaven. There is no such thing as a delay in the Heavenly realm. When you speak, your words are immediately heard in Heaven. When those words align with the word of God that has already been established in Heaven, angels are dispatched to the Earth realm to work on your behalf.

We see an illustration of this in the 10th chapter of the book of Daniel. Daniel was visited by a messenger angel who tells him in verse 12, *"...since the first day you began to pray for understanding and to humble yourself before God, your request has been heard in heaven. I have come in answer to your prayer."* - **(Daniel 10:12 (NLT)**

This scripture teaches us how Heaven begins to move the moment we pray. Our prayers are heard in Heaven and God dispatches angels to the Earth realm. However, the angels sometimes face interference when they enter the Earth realm. Continuing to verse 13, we see the reason the manifestation could be hindered in the Earth.

> *"But for twenty-one days the spirit prince of the kingdom of Persia blocked my way. Then Michael, one of the archangels, came to help me, and I left him there with the*

Introduction

spirit prince of the kingdom of Persia." **-Daniel 10:13 (NLT)**

Based on this scripture we see that once the word has been established in Heaven, it must now be watched over and confessed in the Earth realm until we see manifestation. This is where your legal decrees, (declarations) come into play. Using the scriptural foundation of Daniel 10:13 (NLT), we can declare that the war in the firmaments is turning in our favor. This causes Heaven to spring forth into action AND the Earth realm to do as we command.

You see, Heaven moves at the voice of God, but the Earth moves at the voice of God THROUGH man. In the book of Genesis, God gave man dominion over all the Earth and instructed man to fill the Earth and govern it. (Genesis 1:28 NLT) That means for you to see manifestation in the Earth realm, YOU must use your voice to issue legal decrees. In other words, GOVERN IT with your words!

The Earth does not have free will. Whatever you instruct it to do, it must do. YOU have dominion! You have the power and great responsibility of governing this Earthly realm. When you walk in the fullness of that power, coupled with the faith in what God has spoken to your heart, you are now ready to make fruitful declarations!

Let's recap: Steps to writing effective Affirmations and Declarations

Step 1: Spend time alone with God seeking His response to your questions about your identity. (You show up differently in different areas of life. We'll discuss this in future chapters.)

Step 2: Write down what you heard.

Step 3: Turn what you heard into affirmations, or I AM statements.

Step 4: Search the scriptures for the written word of God that corresponds with what God has spoken.

Step 5: Use your God-given authority to issue legal decrees, or declarations, in the Earth realm.

Life Application:

I remember the day God called me writer. I was crying out to Him in prayer because I didn't understand the financial difficulties I was experiencing. His response to me was, in this season, I called you writer. I was floored. First, I did not fully understand that God would call me different things in different seasons of my life. Second, I had no clue how His response would solve my financial problems. I wanted a job. I'd already written and published five books, but they were not earning enough money to pay the bills. I was lucky if I could afford a cup of coffee off my monthly royalty payments. How was, "I called you writer," a response to my financial problems?

Introduction

Then God spoke to me again, "I called you writer." This time it hit me. I was writing and publishing books, but I did not view myself as a writer. I did not see writing as a revenue stream. I viewed it as something I'd tried and failed at, so I put ZERO stock in being a writer. I wasn't earning a living as a writer, so I did not believe I was one.

Remember, your bank account is always the last one to recognize your success. You can't wait until you physically see money to believe God called you to a thing. You must first activate your faith while walking in full assurance of your call. This means you must DO THE THING even when the thing is not yet producing money. Putting your faith in God and doing as He instructs will ALWAYS lead to provision. In my case, when I stopped looking at what I hadn't earned and added my FAITH to what God said, everything changed!

My affirmation statement became:

I am a writer!

Once I had the faith to believe I was a writer, the next step was to write legal decrees that would cause Heaven and Earth to align with my affirmation statements. Remember, Heaven moves at the word of God. The Earth does not have free will, and you have been given dominion over it. Therefore, the Earth moves at your words. For Heaven and Earth to move on your behalf, you must boldly state what God has told you in complete faith that what you have spoken will come to pass. Armed with this truth, I began writing my legal decrees.

My declarations became:

I decree and declare my writing is sold and read around the world.

I decree and declare my writing creates revenue that helps support my family.

I decree and declare I shall NEVER experience writer's block.

I decree and declare the words I write hold power to set the captives free.

I decree and declare I will always remain an open conduit for the word of God to flow through my fingertips.

I decree and declare I am God's scribe and I write all the words He has given me in a book according to Jeremiah 30:2 (NKJV).

To write my declarations, I took the thoughts of fear that the enemy tried to throw at me and defeated them through the power of my own words. What was once a stumbling block for me became the very thing that helped me move forward in my destiny. Let me be plain, the enemy wanted me to believe no one makes money as a writer, but I knew God wouldn't call me to a profession without provision being attached to it. Therefore, I wrote the decree, "my writing creates revenue that helps support my family." I

Introduction

used the enemy's words against him as I exercised my authority and the Earth obeyed!

The thief does not rob empty houses. You can trust and believe, if he is trying to stop you or make you believe you can't be successful in an area, that is the area which holds the greatest victory for you. Do not bow to fear or any of the other lies of the enemy! Stand firm in your faith AND dominion and let your decrees govern the Earth realm!

Next, I echoed in the Earth realm what had already been decreed and established in Heaven and anchored the declaration in the word of God. As we know, the entire world is held together by the word of God. If it's good enough to hold the world together, it's good enough to anchor my declarations! Amen!!!

Now that we have laid the foundation, I am going to walk you through my 8 personal affirmations that directly correlate to who GOD created me to BE. Remember, it's great to know who you are naturally, but your natural man is not the real you. The real "you" is the spirit God created before the foundations of the world. You are an eternal being living a temporary experience. However, even though this experience is temporary, you are still required to legislate and bring the order and truth of Heaven into the Earth realm. You are called, not to just BE, but to BE, AGREE, and DECREE.

Let's get started...

Affirmation

I am an atmosphere shifter. I operate in the realm of greater works. When I speak, even the winds and waves obey me.

Scripture Reference

"Then Jesus got into the boat and started across the lake with his disciples. Suddenly a fierce storm struck the lake, with waves breaking into the boat. But Jesus was sleeping. The disciples went and woke him up shouting, "Lord, save us! We're going to drown!" Jesus responded, "Why are you afraid? You have so little faith!" Then he got up and rebuked the wind and the waves, and suddenly there was great calm. The disciples were amazed. "Who is this man?" they asked. "Even the winds and waves obey him!" **-Matthew 8:23-27 (NLT)**

Declaration

I decree and declare my words and presence shift the atmosphere of the Earth. The Earth obeys every word I release in Jesus' name!

Chapter 1
I Am an Atmosphere Shifter

Have you ever walked into a room and noticed a shift in the behavior of those already in the room? When I experienced this as a teenager, I immediately assumed those in the room must have been talking about me before I entered. I often felt unliked because of this. I mean, these people called me their friend, so why would they stop talking when I walked in?

Then in my younger adult life, I noticed women in the church I attended were hanging out together, having long phone conversations, traveling together, and forming true friendships. Meanwhile, I liked all of them, but no one wanted to connect with me except for when they wanted me to pray for them. What was wrong with me? Why was I good enough to call for prayer but I wasn't good enough to invite to the birthday party?

This same pattern continued in the workplace. Co-workers laughed and joked with each other. They attended concerts and comedy shows together. During staff meetings, they had inside jokes I knew nothing about, but when there was a work-related question, they asked for my opinion. Why was I good enough to answer work questions, but not good enough to be let in on the inside joke?

Otescia R. Johnson

Before I gained an understanding of who I am, these types of situations were incredibly painful. I felt like I was the person everyone knew from a distance... like a well they knew would always hold water, but never secrets. I can remember when my husband was on his last tour of duty in Afghanistan. Over the years, he'd become my closest and dearest friend because he let me in on all the jokes. I felt like someone he genuinely wanted to be around. While he was gone, I silently cried because I could not physically be with him, and there was no one near me who wanted to be around me. Of course, this was untrue, but it is how I felt.

That day as I sat on my bed and cried out to God, He spoke back to me, "I have to protect your gift. Everyone can't be your friend. When I need to use you to speak into someone's life, they can't question whether it's you speaking or Me speaking. They have to know it is coming from Me, so I cannot allow you to become too familiar with people. I have a set group of friends for you. In time, I will reveal them."

Although I knew I'd heard the voice of God, what He was saying to me did not bring me much comfort. I wanted friends so I wouldn't feel lonely, yet He literally told me He was preventing this from happening. Although I didn't like the response, I knew God only wanted what was best for me, so I dried my tears and made the decision to trust Him.

It would be several years before I grasped the fullness of His response. It happened after He instructed me to start a Facebook group for Kingdom Entrepreneurs. In this

I Am an Atmosphere Shifter

group, God instructed me to teach His people His word as well as practical tips to launching and growing a business. I thought the group would be a place to run a 5-day challenge. I had no clue God was setting me up to reveal even more of my identity to me.

During the initial 5 days of the challenge, God opened His word to me in a way I'd never seen before. He revealed business principles through passages of scripture. He showed me how to teach in a way that brought the Bible into modern analogies which made it easier for the participants to understand the messages. Instantly a shift happened not only in me, but also within those who participated in the challenge.

This community was the birthplace of a new revelation for me: I AM AN ATMOSPHERE SHIFTER.

All those years of not fitting in began to make sense. As God began to use me to accurately prophesy to people, I'd never met before, I watched shy people step out of the shadows. I watched men and women begin to walk in the fullness of their calling. Those who'd struggled to remain locked in during prayer were beginning to consistently tune in to prayer at 5am. Couples whose marriages were previously strained began to wake up and listen together. Atmospheres were shifting in homes just from me showing up as ME and allowing Holy Spirit to speak through me.

About 10 months after this began, God challenged me to come out from the safety of the private community and share some messages publicly. Instantly I wanted to say no.

Otescia R. Johnson

The thought of public scrutiny and judgment settled on me like a cinderblock around my neck. I agonized over it for days until the revelation came. God wasn't asking me to do anything I could not do, nor was He asking me to do anything new. God was asking me to step onto a different platform, but He was always asking for the same thing… for me to just BE ME.

I am an atmosphere shifter whether I am speaking to an empty room, a stadium full of people, or all of Facebook via live video. My responsibility did not change. My assignment did not change. I knew these things were true, but the nagging question at the back of my mind was, why did it feel different? Why were my hands trembling? Why was my heart pounding? Why was I having a negative physical response to the idea of going live publicly with these messages for Kingdom Entrepreneurs, if the assignment had not changed?

The answer came as I talked to my husband about it. He listened to me and watched the tears roll down my cheeks as I described my fears. Finally, as gently and lovingly as you can imagine, he said to me, "You care too much about what people think."

Insert record scratch here…

Wait…. what? That's not at all what I expected him to say. He said some other things after that, but I honestly can't remember a single word. I was too busy rebutting his statement in my mind. I sat mentally arguing with him as he

I Am an Atmosphere Shifter

went on to try to explain his statement. What did that have to do with the fact that God was asking me, the person who has never been to Bible College, to go live to THE PUBLIC and explain Biblical truths about business? Didn't God know how many people had the educational degrees to do this? Why couldn't He call the Bible scholar who could argue anyone down about the merits of the Bible and how to properly interpret scripture? Weren't there people who were called to that? Again… heart racing, hands sweating, eyes wide with fear, face wet with tears, ears tuned out from whatever hubs was saying. I was once again the girl who was afraid people would stop talking when she walked into the room.

Then, a couple days later, God finally got through to me. "Otescia, I've called you. The message is in your belly. People are praying for help to launch and run the businesses I called them to. I want to use you to help them. Can I work through you?"

God really does know how to get through to His children because those words helped me get over myself and yield to His instructions. I came into agreement with the way God saw me. He didn't see me as a small-town girl. He saw me as a woman ordained to shift the atmosphere of nations.

As I agreed with God, I noticed the same atmosphere shifting power released when I went live in the private community, was being released when I went live publicly. People began messaging me letting me know how much they were blessed by my live videos. Testimonies began to pour in from people I have never met in person. Through my agreement with who GOD says I AM, lives were literally changed. This is what happens when you come into agreement with Heaven. Your agreement opens the door for what exists in Heaven to manifest in the Earth.

After I learned how to BE and AGREE, I needed to DECREE. It is not always easy to boldly decree I am an atmosphere shifter. It can be intimidating! I started to wonder what people would think or say about me if they heard me commanding the wind to obey me. In those moments, God reminded me of what my husband said to me, "You care too much about what people think." That is my cue to run to the scriptures.

In Mark 4:39 (NKJV), Jesus made the winds behave by using 3 little words, "Peace be still." Jesus shifted the atmosphere by the power of His words. The Bible teaches us we will do even greater works than those Jesus did. (John 14:12 NKJV) This means, I too can use my words to shift atmospheres. Therefore, if I am attempting to speak in front of what feels like a "cold audience," I can walk into that room and command the atmosphere to shift. If I'm in a business meeting and feel as though I am not being heard or that I am being treated poorly, I can invoke the power of Heaven to come into the room and soften the hearts of the individuals.

As we've previously established, declarations are legal decrees that the Earth has no choice but to obey. When I exercise my authority as an atmosphere shifter and decree

I Am an Atmosphere Shifter

that the winds of favor are blowing to bring favorable conditions as I accomplish what God has sent me to do, that's exactly what must happen. People may not always understand why they want to help me, but they do. They may have 100 more applicants who seemed more qualified than me, yet I am offered the deal. This is because I am who God says I am... an atmosphere shifter. I agree with what Heaven says about me, and I release decrees to ensure the Earth realm comes into alignment with Heaven. I shift the atmospheres of rooms, cities, states, and even nations.

This expression of Holy Spirit through my identity is a pillar of my existence and a linchpin to my success. This means I have a responsibility to walk as I have been called. The mantle of atmosphere shifter rests upon my life so that I can walk out what God has assigned me to do in the Earth. I will experience opposition, but that does not stop me. Instead, I open my mouth and command the winds to come into alignment with what has been established in Heaven.

I am an atmosphere shifter. If you are walking in agreement with Heaven, you are also an atmosphere shifter. I encourage you to settle this truth within yourself. Jesus shifted the atmosphere which means you are called to do the same. This is not something to shy away from. It is your responsibility as a child of the most High and joint heir with Christ. Atmosphere Shifters... assume your position!

BE an atmosphere shifter!

Open your mouth and AGREE with Heaven as you state, "I am an atmosphere shifter"!

Otescia R. Johnson

Use your dominion and authority over the Earth to issue a legal DECREE. The winds hear and obey the sound of my voice according to Mark 4:39 NKJV.

Affirmation

I am accepted. Jesus loves and accepts all of me. He satisfies my hunger and thirst.

Scripture Reference

"Jesus replied, "I am the bread of life. Whoever comes to me will never be hungry again. Whoever believes in me will never be thirsty. But you haven't believed in me even though you have seen me. However, those the Father has given me will come to me, and I will never reject them." - **John 6:35-38 (NLT)**

Declaration

I decree and declare I am accepted in all rooms, by all people God has ordained for my life! I curse the fear of rejection and receive the acceptance of God in the Earth realm daily. My interactions with other men and women are blessed according to God's perfect plan for my life.

Chapter 2
I Am Accepted

This chapter may be a little more difficult for some to digest. That's okay. We'll take this one nice and slow, so that we remain on the same page. How does that sound? Let's begin.

Remember last chapter when I explained to you, I was always the person on the outside of the inside jokes? Well, as you can imagine, this led to a serious case of rejection anxiety. I'm not sure if that is a medical term or not, but it's what I call it. Because I did not feel people really wanted to hear what I had to say beyond the very direct and surface level questions they asked me, I developed anxiety around new people. I had a gift of spotting ways to improve systems and processes at work, but I lacked the experience and wisdom to present those ideas properly. As a result, in those rare moments I when I did speak up, I often offended and upset people. Well, when you go through this enough, in both your private and professional life, you eventually learn to just be quiet.

In my early 20's, I stopped speaking up in new environments. The sassy bold woman I am now was insecurely tucked away behind the mask of timidity I wore for the world. I silenced her. I told her she was problematic and judgmental. I told her she needed to learn how to keep her mouth shut and stop trying to help when she hadn't been asked her opinion. I willingly gave way to the anxiety and fear of rejection that the enemy offered me. Instead of realizing my identity as a forerunner means I can see future trends before others, I told myself I needed to learn to shut up until they asked for my opinion.

It took years of intimacy with God to identify these patterns of thoughts and behaviors. I was living in Germany in 2008, when God started to dismantle my rejection anxiety. I was led to volunteer at the Chapel. There was a new service at 1pm on Sundays called the Gospel Service, led by a man I can only describe as being best friends with Holy Spirit. He was purposefully different. He'd lead spontaneous worship medleys with a hint of the Caribbean even though he wasn't from the islands. He taught calmly and methodically. He didn't jump around or "preach" hard like I was accustomed to. He didn't bust out in unknown tongues during service. I'd never met anyone like him, but God revealed this man's heart to me. He had a love and devotion to God I'd never seen before. God whispered to me, "Help him. Serve here."

God's instruction was like a breath of fresh air on one hand, because I'd been praying for a ministry to attend for six months. On the other hand, I was nervous because it seemed like those who were attending the service were babes. If you aren't familiar with this term, babe is used to describe someone who is at the beginning of their relationship with God. At that time, I felt like I was more

I Am Accepted

mature, and I wanted to experience a connection with other mature Believers. Yet, God had a plan for me there.

Under the leadership of this Pastor, I developed a deeper longing to please God. I spent hours in prayer, reading my Bible, and just communing with Holy Spirit. As time progressed, the Pastor assembled all the volunteers for a dinner. He stressed we should know those we were laboring among. I attended the dinner with the full intent of remaining silent. I wasn't willing to open up and risk being judged or rejected, so I sat silently as two of the women at the table chatted away.

One of those ladies grabbed my cell phone that night and entered her name and phone number. I seriously thought she was a little off her rocker, no matter how sweet she appeared to be. Who just grabs someone's phone and puts their number in there? No one I had any intentions of calling!

All of this transpired on a Friday night. That Monday when I woke up, I noticed I had a headache. It was mild, but a headache, nonetheless. When I went to get ready for work, I noticed I had small red spots on the right side of my forehead. I thought "…it's an allergic reaction to something." So, I decided not to put on my foundation. I just washed my face and continued getting ready for work. By the middle of the day my head felt like someone was bashing it with a hammer. I spoke to my supervisor and told her I needed to go home. She noticed the red spots had grown larger and were now raised. We weren't sure what was wrong with me, but we agreed I needed to go home.

By the time I picked up my children and drove home, the corner of my right eye hurt every time I blinked. By bedtime, my eye was so itchy I felt like I was going to claw my own eye out. I'd taken pain medicine, but my head still felt like it was going to explode and the spots on my face were all painful to the touch.

When I woke up on Tuesday morning, my eye was crusted shut and I immediately thought I must have pink eye. I couldn't explain the headache or the spots, but I knew I needed to be seen. I took the children to school and scheduled an appointment with the doctor. By the time I got to the doctor's office, my eye was starting to swell, and I felt totally exhausted. The doctor took one look at me and revealed I had Shingles. I thought shingles was an "old person's disease." The mere thought of me having Shingles was crazy.

The next thing he said scared me. "Your eye doesn't look good. If this thing gets into your eye, it can damage your cornea. You'd lose your vision."

Stunned to silence, the doctor led me to the other side of the clinic to see the eye doctor. So many thoughts ran through my mind as the two professionals discussed my case. I knew it was odd for two doctors to talk directly instead of going through nurses or emailing, but they both seemed very worried about me. I sat silently trying to

I Am Accepted

understand what they were discussing as the pounding in my head interrupted my focus.

My primary care doctor eventually left the room as the eye doctor took over. He examined me and revealed there was a concerning spot on my cornea. He stressed how important it was for me to take the drops he was prescribing. Though he tried to remain calm, there was panic in his voice. He asked if I had anyone to help me. I informed him my husband was deployed to Iraq and I didn't have any close friends. I wasn't sure who would help me. He listened but stressed I would need help and that I would need to come to his office every day so he could track my eye's progress. I had a very short window to attack the spot with the eye drops before the damage would be permanent and cause me to lose vision in that eye.

I drove home afraid, in pain, and confused. Who would help me with my children? Who would take me to the doctor every day? Who would take the children to school and pick them up? How was I supposed to stay away from others? When I arrived home, God reminded me of the woman who put her phone number into my phone. He said, "Call her."

Remember, I suffered from rejection anxiety, but I literally had no one else to turn to. My family members were all in other countries. I had to trust God and this woman I did not know. Despite my fear, I called the woman and explained I needed help. She asked me what I needed her to do, and I only asked her to pick the children up for me.

She then asked me how I was going to get to the doctor every day. I told her since it was only 3 blocks away, I'd drive myself. She insisted on driving me, and I agreed.

Next, I needed to have help getting the children to school. God reminded me of my neighbor who lived directly in front of me. Our children were very close in age. He told me to write her a note asking her to call me. I wrote the note and had my daughter deliver it to her. She called me right away.

Again, despite my fear of being rejected, I asked if she'd take my children to school. She quickly agreed, told me what time to have the children meet her outside, and ended the call. I didn't get the warm and fuzzies, but I didn't get rejected either, which was more than enough for me.

That afternoon, I received a call from the pastor. The woman from church had called and let him know I was sick. He prayed for me and let me know I wasn't alone. Up until this point, I'd only had a handful of conversations with him. I was so moved that he took the time to call and pray for me... a woman he barely knew.

Then around 6pm there was a knock at the door. A different lady from church was there to drop off dinner for me and the children. I was so shocked. I'd never seen this type of love and support before. I'd never heard of a "meal train," but one was organized for me. Every day the women of that church, along with my neighbor, made sure the children and I were fed and well taken care of.

I Am Accepted

On Thursday, I was so exhausted from being in constant pain despite taking strong painkillers every 4 hours. When I went to the eye doctor that day, I told him I didn't know how much longer I could handle the constant pain. My entire face was swollen. My right eye was swollen shut and every time he pried it open to examine it, I felt like someone was stabbing me in the eye with a knife.

This time, he left to go get my primary care doctor. The spot on my cornea was clearing up but everything else was worse. The white of my eye had turned a dark gray looking color, and my entire face felt like it was on fire. When my primary care doctor came into the room, he halted at my appearance. He tried to hide his shock, but I knew he was wondering how in the world I'd gotten so much worse in just a few days. They stepped out in the hall to talk. They closed the door, but I knew they were talking about how bad I looked. I sat there silently praying and crying. I felt battle fatigued and weary.

When they re-entered the room, the primary care doctor explained he was sending me for more bloodwork because I should have been getting better, not worse. In fact, both doctors told me they'd never seen a case like mine. I didn't have a response for their statements, so I simply nodded as I headed towards the lab to have my blood drawn. The woman from church stayed with me the whole time and chatted away while I struggled to hold back tears. She was speaking so much positivity over me in those moments. I was just in too much pain to process what was happening.

Otescia R. Johnson

Because my appearance was so bad, I wore a hat pulled low and sunglasses to try to hide how terrible I looked. I later learned my efforts were futile. Months later, while taking my children for their routine immunizations, it was revealed to me that it was assumed I was a battered woman. Imagine that! People thought my husband (who would never abuse me by the way AND who wasn't even in the country) was abusing me. Yet NO ONE at the clinic came to my aid or even bothered to try to figure out who I was so that I could be helped. That news really hurt me.

Back to the story at hand… While we were waiting for my blood to be drawn, my primary care doctor came over and told me he was prescribing me a new medication. He told me to stop taking the other one and start the new one immediately. He said the new one rarely worked, but he knew we had to try something different. He'd also scheduled an appointment for me to see him the following day, which was Friday. So not only would this woman I'd only known for a week have to drive me to one appointment, but she'd also have to wait while I had both appointments. I tried to raise my concerns, but she cut me off and told the doctor she would be there.

That night after the meal was delivered and the children had eaten and bathed, all on their own (my oldest was only in 6th grade but he stepped up to help his younger siblings), I lay in bed and asked God to heal me. I told Him the doctors were confused, but I knew He could baffle them with how

I Am Accepted

quickly I would get better. I drifted off to sleep with that prayer echoing in my heart, mind, and spirit.

Baffle the doctors…

Baffle the doctors…

Baffle the doctors…

When I woke up on Friday morning, the headache was completely gone. It was as if it never happened. I went into the bathroom and smiled at my less swollen face. I could actually open my eye. It still looked bad, but I had energy and ZERO pain!

When my ride for the doctor came, I smiled at her, and she returned it with a broad smile of her own. We both celebrated and praised God! This time, I was the one chatting away, completely forgetting about my rejection anxiety. I talked her head off as we drove to the clinic and waited for my name to be called.

When I went into the eye doctor's exam room, he shut the door behind him as he typically did and asked, "How are you feeling?"

I shot up in my seat for the first time all week and proclaimed, "I feel great! My head doesn't hurt at all."

He replied, "Well praise the Lord!!!"

"Yes!!!!!" I screamed! "Praise Him because I prayed hard, He'd baffle the doctors with how quickly He healed me."

Otescia R. Johnson

The doctor laughed loudly and said, "Well, He heard you because I planned to admit you to the hospital today. You were too sick to go the whole weekend without being seen. I spent most of the night chatting with doctors online trying to figure out your case, and the consensus was you needed to be admitted."

"Oh no, I can't go to the hospital. Who's gonna watch my kids?"

"Well, now that you're better you don't have to go. Just let me examine your eye to confirm the spot is gone."

Reader, I need you to fully understand what happened. I went from feeling like death Monday – Thursday to zero pain on Friday! When I saw my primary care doctor that day, he explained that, in addition to Shingles, I was having an allergic reaction to the first medicine he prescribed. He said it made no medical sense that I got better because what he gave me typically does not work. That's why he didn't initially prescribe it, but he didn't know what else to do after seeing how bad I was the previous day.

That was the doctor's medical explanation, but I knew a spiritual battle had just been won. That day, instead of driving me home and leaving, the woman from church, Ms. EJ Cole, came inside my home and sat with me for hours. We laughed, joked, and became instant best friends. After all, this was the first day she was actually getting to meet ME. Previously, I'd remained silent, only calling her out of

I Am Accepted

need and obedience. I'd held my thoughts and personality inside, effectively not giving her anything to connect with.

This day, I was so grateful to God for healing me that I just couldn't shut up! I blabbed and blabbed and blabbed some more. We learned we were over 2 decades apart in age, but we had so many things in common. She was hilarious and could literally brighten up ANY room. She loved God deeply and loved bringing people together. Before she left that day, she asked me to speak at a women's gathering she was hosting at the Chapel. She asked me to speak about what it means to be a wife. In my giddy state, I agreed without even considering the possibility of being rejected.

Two weeks later, it was time for the event. My face still held the scars from my ordeal and my right eye was still smaller than the left one. A specialist told me I had nerve damage from Shingles, and my eye lid would always droop. If you've seen a picture of me, you know God baffled the doctors with that one as well. As I stood in front of those women that day with my little eye and face scarred from Shingles, I poured out my heart. I was naked and vulnerable. I didn't share the cute little message I'd prepared. I shared my story, the good, the bad, and the ugly, just as God instructed me to do minutes before we started.

I shared without fear of rejection. I shared out of obedience to God, but what I got in return was God's gift to me. When I finished speaking, the women embraced me. They not only listened, but they identified with me. They celebrated my courage instead of judging me. It was the first time I walked away from an event feeling totally accepted. Not only accepted and approved by God but accepted by those He loves.

I wanted to share the fullness of that experience with you to reveal a few things. First, I had to BE accepted, meaning I had to walk into a room in the power of God's acceptance. I had to BE His servant, His chosen vessel, and His voice. I transitioned from overthinking and shying away from offering suggestions to boldly walking IN acceptance.

Next, I had to spend the next few months agreeing with Heaven regarding my acceptance. This led to me taking over as the leader of the women's ministry after my friend transitioned back to the States. Because I'd already learned to BE accepted, it was an easy transition to agree with that acceptance. I stopped saying things like, "I can't believe God chose me to lead His daughters." Instead, I started saying, "God knew everything I would do before I did it and He still chose me."

God chose me because He accepted me, flaws, and all. Because God accepted me, His daughters accepted me. Because God and His daughters accepted me, I embraced and accepted me! It's true that my issues with rejection were rooted in real experiences, but those experiences were not in alignment with my true identity of acceptance. When I let go of the fear of rejection, I came into agreement with Heaven's acceptance, which empowered me to issue legal decrees about my acceptance.

I Am Accepted

I decree and declare my voice goes out and accomplishes that which God has sent it to accomplish (Isaiah 55:11 NKJV).

I decree and declare my audience knows my voice and hearkens to my frequency as I tell them about the goodness of Jesus.

I decree and declare that Otescia Johnson is a household name, and as they call me, I make His name great.

I decree and declare that when I speak, others listen.

I decree and declare rejection is destroyed in my life and will never stop me from completing my assignment ever again.

I am accepted and Reader… and so are you!

Affirmation

I am wealthy. I am well provided for. It is God's pleasure to bless me.

Scripture Reference

"And my God shall supply all your need according to His riches in glory by Christ Jesus." **-Philippians 4:19 (NKJV)**

Declaration

I decree and declare I am wealthy. The entire Earth is conspiring to deliver wealth into my hands daily. Heaven is releasing my supply now and I readily receive it in Jesus' name. No demonic force or spirit can interfere with, block, stop, or hinder the supernatural flow of God's provision in my life. I receive wealth and abundance from Heaven now, in Jesus' name!

Chapter 3
I Am Wealthy

Wealth- *The measure of all the valuable resources under one's control.* (Investopedia)

As a child who was born into impoverished conditions, saying I am wealthy did not come easy for me. It simply was not a part of what I perceived as my identity. If you've read the first book of this series, you already know how financially strained my childhood was. When God began using me to preach, I identified myself in sermons as a little poor girl from South Carolina. The fact that God was using me to proclaim the Gospel to women from different cultural backgrounds, socio-economic statuses, and countries was totally insignificant to me.

To acknowledge the way God was using me would mean I'd have to divorce my identity as the little poor girl. If I wasn't her, who would I be? When it came to my identity, my past was all I was sure of. I was accustomed to the poor girl who was teased for not looking, dressing, and sounding like the popular kids. If I was no longer her, who was I?

Otescia R. Johnson

Surely, I couldn't think too highly of myself and start believing I was somehow chosen to step out of the shadows of social obscurity. That would be arrogance... wouldn't it? Even though I have always had less than my peers, I'm prone to arrogance... aren't I? Others have said I was arrogant, so it must be true. These questions plagued me constantly for years. So much so, I self-sabotaged myself on several occasions.

One of the occasions happened at an event where I was the keynote speaker. There I was on the flyer with people who had a much larger following than my own. They'd been on television. They were well known, with recognizable names, and I literally stood on stage and identified myself as "the girl next door, the little poor girl from South Carolina."

When the event was over, the other two speakers spoke among themselves and discussed working together in the future. I was right there next to them, but I did not open my mouth to speak to either of them or any of the attendees approaching us. Instead, I took a seat and waited for the event organizer to invite the speakers to take pictures. After the pictures, I went to my vendor table, packed up my belongings, and left with the person who'd attended the event with me.

On the ride home, I thought about what happened. I felt slighted, like an outsider ignored by the popular kids. It felt like Elementary School all over again... the days when being me meant being overlooked and only spoken to so that the popular kids would have someone to laugh at later.

I Am Wealthy

It took me a while to recognize what actually took place that night.

The other two speakers did exactly what they were supposed to do following an event. They networked. They bonded with another person in their industry in hopes of forming a mutually beneficial relationship. I, on the other hand, sat silently watching it all unfold because I did not identify as a wealthy woman who belonged in the conversation. They didn't exclude me, I excluded myself.

The fact of the matter was, one of the ladies was a host, the other was a psalmist. I WAS THE KEYNOTE SPEAKER. Yet, I walked into the room like the pauper who didn't belong at the table with royalty. I presented myself as standoffish and unapproachable because I was uncomfortable with their perceived wealth. I was uncomfortable with their perceived wealth because despite how far I was from poverty, and the overwhelming number of prophecies I've received about wealth, I never divorced the false identity of the little poor girl.

Late 2020, I was introduced to Pastor Clyde Lewis, one of the most influential and transformational people I've ever met. Pastor Clyde specialized in identity coaching and offered to coach me through 5 identity coaching sessions. By this point, after being corrected by Holy Spirit, I'd stopped calling myself the little poor girl. However, despite the fact that the words were no longer spoken, I never divorced that identity. I didn't even KNOW it was an identity. So, while I was seeing financial increase, I knew I still hadn't reached my full potential.

During the very first coaching session, Pastor Clyde helped me to see the root of my issue was the false identity of poverty. Instead of being wealthy, I'd developed habits of self-promotion, self-provision, and self-protection. Every time I faced a money issue, it would stop me in my tracks. I'd cry out to God and throw spiritual temper tantrums. If you're not familiar with this term, imagine a grown woman sitting on the floor feeling sorry for herself while crying and begging God to "finally" end the cycle of poverty between her bouts of panic and worry. Immediately following the temper tantrum, I'd get up, wash my face, then go into beast mode. "I know how to make money," I'd say aloud to myself. "Stop crying girl. You got this. Go be great!"

Pastor Clyde helped me to see I wasn't trusting God to be my provider. I was toiling to provide for myself which left me burnt out and consistently vacillating between not having enough to having just enough. No matter what I tried, I just couldn't seem to earn past a certain level.

I want to give you a practical example of what it looks like to attempt to provide for yourself, instead of trusting God to be your provider. Years ago, God began talking to me about trusting Him to be my provider. I would say I trusted God, but every time a money issue popped up, I would panic, become extremely stressed out, cry, and throw the temper tantrum I mentioned earlier. I was so afraid of not

I Am Wealthy

having enough and losing everything that I'd immediately begin trying to solve my own problem.

I'd create some sort of offer, course, or program that would in fact sell, or following up with leads I hadn't heard from to see if they were still interested in moving forward. Like clockwork, money would come in and the need would be met. While this cycle seemed to have worked, it was emotionally and spiritually exhausting. Each phase of the cycle left me feeling like I couldn't catch my breath. It took more and more effort and energy to keep going until I finally just couldn't do it any longer.

At that time, I didn't know I could simply seek the things of God and ask Holy Spirit to reveal the solution to me. The Bible teaches us in Matthew 6:25-33 (NLT) not to worry about everyday life because if we seek the Kingdom of God above all else, He will give us everything we need. I'd read and quoted this scripture many times, but I had no revelation of how to actually live this way. So, instead of following Heaven's direction for provision, I did things like getting personal loans, payday advances, maxing out credit cards, and taking on business projects that left me burnt out and frustrated.

None of these things made my situation better. In fact, they made them worse. After working with Pastor Clyde, I learned how to lean into Holy Spirit for solutions instead of practicing those old habits tied to the false identity of poverty. I began to understand I no longer needed to self-promote or self-protect because God desired to care for me as His daughter. I rejected the urges to take matters into my own hands when financial needs arose. Instead, I began to pray the following:

"God, I thank you for taking care of me and paying this bill. You said you would supply all my need according to Your riches in glory. I thank you for supernatural provision to take care of this need."

As a result of these changes, I quickly blew through all previous earning ceilings. Within 3 months, my business earned more than the previous six months. All of this happened because I learned to do one simple thing, BE WEALTHY. Before walking this road, I thought being wealthy was about the amount of money in my bank account. I now understand nothing could be further from the truth.

Being wealthy is a state of mind in which I understand I have been given dominion over the Earth and all its resources. It involves letting go of my fears concerning lack and embracing the fact that God has already provided everything I will ever need. There is no such thing as a debt Heaven cannot pay. There is no bill God will not either give you grace to extend the due date, give you the money to pay, or completely eradicate. To be wealthy is to rest in the knowledge that you have a promise of provision.

> *"And my God shall supply all your need according to His riches in glory by Christ Jesus."* **-Philippians 4:19 NKJV**

I Am Wealthy

Early this year, God began dealing with me about inheritance. From a natural perspective, I know the chances of me receiving an inheritance from my parents are slim to none. Yet, God would not let up about the inheritance I have access to. When I began to inquire more about what He was referring to, He gave me the following.

The Reading of the Will

Each person of the Godhead (God, Jesus, Holy Spirit) has a unique responsibility and role to play in the life of the Believer. When God rested on the 7th day, He finished His job. When Jesus ascended into Heaven after His death, burial, and resurrection, He finished His job. From the time Holy Spirit entered the Earth realm until now, He has been on His job. Holy Spirit's job is to be our counselor in the Earth and to reveal that which God has for us.

The life and teachings of Jesus Christ gave us the ability to be adopted into the family of God. When our big brother Jesus gave up the ghost, He also unlocked our spiritual inheritance. He unlocked everything we have access to in the spirit realm. From the time Holy Spirit entered the Earth until the day Jesus returns, Holy Spirit's assignment has been to reveal to us exactly what it means to be a joint heir with Christ.

When someone dies in the natural, the family gathers to hear the reading of the will so everyone will know what has been given to them. Holy Spirit has been reading the will to us for decades. He's been revealing everything that has been given to us by God, the Father. This is the longest reading of the will the world will ever know because as long as you are breathing, Holy Spirit will keep reading. Every day He desires to share another gift, benefit, and ability with you.

Since we know God is the owner of the whole world, we know our inheritance (the valuable resources under our control) includes all the wealth and riches the Earth can hold. When you tap into this inheritance, you tap into the wealth that has been prepared for you. You do not have to work your way into this. It has been willed to you. It already BELONGS to you. You must simply acknowledge and receive your inheritance. You were MADE wealthy and are receiving new benefits DAILY!

Wealth Confession:

I am wealthy because God made me wealthy. I have more than enough. My seeds are producing a harvest for me daily. I decree and declare the wealth of the wicked has been laid up for me and all of Heaven and Earth are conspiring to bring that wealth to me daily.

> *"Wealth is an identity, not a status. It points to who you are, not what you have. Money does not make you wealthy; money is a result of being wealthy."* -Lyndell Johnson

I Am Wealthy

Remember, you have been called to BE what God has already called you. Your bank account is always the last one to realize how wealthy you are, so do not limit your belief to what your bank account holds. Instead, walk in the assurance of the provision of your God. Move as though you have access to the bank of Heaven because you do!

Then, when you speak of yourself, AGREE with what Heaven has said. Use the wealth confession in this chapter to help you until you are able to write your own. Finally, write out and verbally issue your legal decrees concerning your wealth. Be detailed and specific according to scripture. The Bible is full of wealth promises. Remember you can have anything written from Genesis to Revelations. This is God's will concerning you. He never intended for you to live a life of struggle. You are of the lineage of Abraham, which means you can still pull on those promises. Research what God promised to Abraham and his descendants. Read what God said about provision in the New Testament, then allow the Holy Spirit to guide you as you write your wealth declarations. Recite them aloud daily so that the Earth has the instructions it needs to bring your wealth to you. Remember, you have dominion for a reason… USE IT!

Affirmation

I am a prayer warrior. When I pray, all of Heaven stands ready to take action. I win spiritual battles through the power of my prayers.

Scripture Reference

"Confess your sins to teach each other and pray for each other so that you may be healed. The earnest prayer of a righteous person has great power and produces wonderful results." **-James 5:16 (NLT)**

Declaration

I decree and declare I am a powerful prayer warrior. My prayers are powerful and produce mighty results. My prayers bring order, give instruction, and provide direction as the will of God is released through me in the Earth realm!

Chapter 4
I am a Prayer Warrior

I was 16 years old when I got the "urge" to pray. The older members of my family would probaby laugh at this statement and say my prayers started when I was much younger and attempted to get out of being disciplined. It has been said I could pray really hard for God to "talk to my mother" so she would not spank me. Of course, I can't recall this but in truth, it sounds like something I would do.

In my early teens, my parents, encouraged by my mother's best friend, began having what they referred to as family prayer. During this time, we'd all have to get on our knees in the living room as they "tarried." If you aren't from the Southern United States, you may not be familiar with this terminology, so I'll explain it to you. This type of prayer consists of lots of crying and calling on the Holy Spirit during an undetermined amount of time because we couldn't "rush" God. All the adults would take their turns praying aloud, yelling loud enough for all of Heaven to hear them as they made their requests known. By the time everyone finished, we'd be sweating from the heat and excursion. I didn't understand what was happening during those prayers, but I did enjoy them, and I "felt" something. My mother told me what I felt was the presence of God, but I had no clue what she meant, and she didn't know how to explain it to me.

Because of my lack of understanding, it would be another 3-4 years before I actually wanted to pray. When I was 16, my family started attending a new church. It was at that church that I saw so many women who could pray so powerfully that I felt moved to want to do the same. There was a fire in their prayers that made me feel like they got God's attention. It wasn't about yelling, or sweating, or even tarrying. It was just the sincerity and power of their words.

One Sunday, I heard the Pastor say, "This is a powerful woman of prayer. She is a prayer warrior." That was it! I had a word for what I wanted to be. You know how everyone asks teenagers what they want to be when they grow up? For years I'd said I wanted to be a lawyer or teacher, but I wasn't passionate about either of those things. I just knew I'd be good at them based on what adults told me over the years. But this…. this prayer warrior thing… that interested me! I could absolutely be a person who could get all of Heaven to listen as she prayed.

I looked at the woman the Pastor spoke to in awe. I had no idea how she became a prayer warrior, but I wanted to learn. However, that pesky fear of rejection was very much alive and active in my life at the time, so I never asked her to teach me. I just watched her every chance I got. I listened carefully as she prayed. I watched her posture. I listened when she spoke and realized the weirdest thing to my teenage mind. She was soft-spoken. This woman who was

I Am a Prayer Warrior

calling on Heaven with authority and great boldness was as timid as could be when she wasn't praying. She'd learned how to go boldly before the throne of grace, but in her normal speaking voice she was gentle and a little shy.

The church was pastored by a couple who both moved heavily in the prophetic. The husband was the Senior Pastor, and the wife was the Co-Pastor. They alternated preaching and teaching duties. Both were powerful in their own right, but the wife was someone I also admired. Just like the woman who was proclaimed to be a prayer warrior, she was able to pray boldly and proclaim the gospel with great authority, but outside of those times, she was very kind and gentle. She was soft-spoken and rarely raised her voice, in my presence. Again…there were those qualities glaring at me, shy, soft-spoken, gentle.

I didn't consider myself to be gentle or shy. The adults around me had told me many things about my personality, and those words had never been a part of the conversation. So, after watching these two women, I determined I must not have been prayer warrior material. In those days, we had a weekly Friday night service. By my 18th birthday, I was attending every single service. I never missed a Friday night. While my peers were partying, I was at church. It was my happy place.

I often arrived at service a little early. The Overseer of the church, Reverend Betty Jones was our officiate for every service. She'd ask different members to read a scripture or pray. Arriving early meant, I was in view to be asked to participate in the service. I didn't mind reading the scripture, so all was well. Then one day, she changed it up and asked me to pray. Me?!?! Pray in front of the whole church? Absolutely NOT! That's what I thought. In truth, I did not realize I could say no. I thought the question was a formality. I was always taught to do what adults told me to do. Whether they framed it as a question or statement was irrelevant, I was expected to do it. Saying no would be disrespectful, so I simply replied, "Yes ma'am."

When it was time for me to pray, I walked to the microphone on wobbly legs. I was so nervous; the microphone shook in my hands. I'd never prayed out loud in church before. Heck, I prayed inwardly at home when I was alone, now I was being asked to pray in front of everyone! I just KNEW I was going to sound ridiculous. I couldn't pray as powerfully as the women I admired. No one would feel the presence of God when I prayed.

I stood there terrified as all eyes were on me. I decided looking back at them was a terrible idea, so I closed my eyes and opened my mouth. I can't tell you what happened next because I don't know. All I know is by the time I said amen, others were saying amen as well. There was clapping. There were hallelujahs, and other words of praise. I'd survived and it seemed like everyone was okay with what was said.

I was relieved the moment was over as I took my seat and collected myself. My heart was pounding in my ears, but I'd survived. Surely, she wouldn't ever ask me to do that again, I thought to myself. I was wrong. Week after week, I was

I Am a Prayer Warrior

asked to pray during the Friday night service. You would think my nerves calmed down…. they did not! I was equally nervous each time she called my name.

One week, I was so over all the anxiety and nerves that I decided to show up to service late so she would not be able to ask me to pray before service began. I was confident she would have already asked someone else before I showed up. I got to the service just as they began singing the opening song. I sat down in my usual seat on the third row and began singing along. After the song, she had someone read the scripture. Then it was time for prayer. I stood there waiting to hear who she'd chosen, and this sweet little lady said, "Sis. Otescia, please come lead us in prayer."

What in the whole world is going on?!?!? How am I still being called? She didn't ask me before service. Yet, there I was on the spot in front of everyone. My nerves were more rattled because I wasn't prepared to hear my name called. I couldn't say no, so I just nodded my head and walked to the microphone as I'd done so many times before. I closed my eyes and began to pray, but this time something else happened. I felt the power of God flowing through me in a way I'd never experienced before. I was the one everyone could see, but it was not me praying. For the first time, I realized, what had been happening all along. When I opened my mouth, God filled it!

Otescia R. Johnson

"For it was I, the Lord your God, who rescued you from the land of Egypt. Open your mouth wide, and I will fill it with good things." - **Psalms 81:10 NLT**

From the moment, God formed me in my mother's womb, He created me as a prayer warrior. To walk in the fullness of His creation, I had to start BEING a prayer warrior. Over the next few decades, God began to shape my prayer life by placing me under the tutelage of men and women who spent quality time in prayer. Eventually I stopped trying to become a prayer warrior and simply walked in the truth of my existence.

I could fill a whole book with the results of my prayer life. But for the sake of time, I will share just a few of the results with you. The Bible tells us we defeat the enemy by the blood of the lamb and by our testimony. (Revelation 12:11 NLT) My prayer is for my testimonies to encourage you to walk in the fullness of your existence as the prayer warrior you ARE.

Prayer to land a plane

Late Thanksgiving night in 2008, I received a call from a friend of mine informing me there was a flight to the Eastern United States from Germany, but we'd have to leave right away. After talking it over with my husband, we packed and headed to the Airbase to catch a space available military flight. If you are not familiar with these flights,

I Am a Prayer Warrior

service members and their families are allowed to travel on military air crafts on a "space available" basis. I'd taken a few of these flights previously with no issues, so I didn't expect to have any issues that night.

We all boarded the plane ready for the 8-hour flight to the States. This particular plane was very different from the ones we'd traveled on previously. The seats were backwards, so it felt like we were flying backwards the entire flight. That part didn't bother us very much though because it was late. So once the lights were dimmed, we all went to sleep. About 45 minutes prior to landing, the lights were raised, waking us all. We were given customs forms so that we could declare any items we were bringing into the United States for which we might need to pay taxes. If you've ever flown internationally, you know this form is a welcomed sight because it means your flight is nearly over.

We filled out our forms and waited for landing. After about half an hour we felt the plane dip and rise back up to a higher altitude. I didn't pay it much attention, because I wasn't sure if we were trying to avoid some sort of bad weather. Again, we were extremely exhausted, so we all started to drift back off to sleep. I was awakened when the plane once again dipped down, but this time popped back up a little too quickly.

I looked over to see my teenage son, as well as my friend's son, both holding air sick bags in their hands. Both had gotten sick from the motion of the plane. I looked at my watch and realized more than an hour and half had passed since we were given the customs forms.

"Something is wrong with the plane. Pray."

Those were the instructions Holy Spirit whispered to my heart. I closed my eyes and began to pray inwardly in my Heavenly language. All those years of being too nervous to pray aloud came in handy because I was now able to pray fervently without ever opening my mouth. I began to speak to the plane and command it to work properly. I commanded the angels to guide the plane to a safe landing. I asked God for His favor and protection for all of us on the plane.

As I prayed, my friend's husband went to ask what was going on. The Flight Commander told us the landing gear on the plane was stuck and that they were not sure how they were going to get it down, but they were still working on it. He tried to encourage everyone not to be worried, but you could feel the anxiety begin to rise amongst the passengers. I closed my eyes and returned to my prayer. I didn't talk to anyone except God. I knew He was going to save us. I didn't know how. I didn't care how. I just knew God had me praying for a reason.

Thirty minutes later the Flight Commander made another announcement. He told us the landing gear was now down, but they still weren't sure what was wrong with it, so they could not shut the engines off as we exited the plane. Military Aircrafts are much louder than commercial planes,

I Am a Prayer Warrior

so we were already wearing ear protection. Typically, we are allowed to remove that protection once we land, but we were instructed to keep our ear protection on because they could not shut the plane's engines off.

When we landed, the plane erupted into applause and cheers. I neither clapped nor cheered. I wasn't surprised. I knew God had me on that plane to pray and He'd answered that prayer. The purpose of my family being on that flight went much deeper than a trip to visit family for the holidays. God had me there to pray for everyone… the flight crew, the other families, the Marines flying home from Afghanistan. That entire flight was a prayer assignment for me.

While I wasn't surprised when we landed safely, I was surprised to see what was waiting for us when we exited the plane. We were not allowed to taxi to the terminal for fear of the safety of everyone inside. Instead, they parked us at the far end of a tarmac. They rolled a set of stairs to the door of the plane for us to exit. When I stepped down onto that first step, I looked around at the scene before me. It looked like something out of a movie. There were fire trucks and men in hazmat suits everywhere. There were buses waiting to drive us to the terminal, but you could tell the buses were a late addition due to their positioning. It was still dark outside except for all the lights coming from the fire trucks.

"They were preparing for a crash," Holy Spirit said to me.

Otescia R. Johnson

I smiled as I exited the plane knowing God had done what man could not understand. While the crews were appropriate in their response to the emergency, they did not know there was a prayer warrior on that plane ensuring a safe landing. When we all got onto the bus, I leaned over and whispered to my husband, "They were preparing to scrape us off the tarmac, but God is faithful." Apparently, I did not whisper as softly as I thought because one of the Marines behind me said, "This has been the most bizarre trip home. We've been trying to get home for over a week and now this happens."

"But you made it," I replied.

I sat back in my seat and let the weight of what happened sink in. God had my family to jump on a flight we never intended to take just so He could save the lives of the Marines who had been trying to get home safely. He used me in that moment to bring His will into the Earth.

Prayer for a Home

In December 2009, my husband and I were preparing to move back to the United States. We knew my husband would be going to Afghanistan the following year and afterwards he planned to exit the Army. It was essential that the children and I return to the States to get settled before he transitioned to civilian life. We thought we'd be moving back to Georgia which is where we lived prior to being sent to Germany. We sat in our bed, each on our laptops,

I Am a Prayer Warrior

looking for a home, but nothing seemed to be right. After a couple days of this, I went to God in prayer.

"Lord, why aren't we able to find a home?"

"You never asked me where to go."

"Lord, I'm afraid to ask You where to go. You might tell us to go to California or somewhere."

I must note here, I was afraid of living in California. In my mind, it was a God-less place filled with all types of immoral people. I have no idea where that judgment came from, but years later, God did send my family and me to California. He tore down all of those false beliefs and revealed Himself to me in ways I'd never experienced. God will never allow us to keep monuments to fear and pain in our hearts. Whatever you fear, you must face so that you can see He is God over that as well.

It took me a few days to get the courage to ask God where to move. But when I did, He readily responded with North Carolina. I was shocked. I'd lived in North Carolina for years. It was home for me, but I did not want to live there. Out of obedience though, I went to my husband and told him what God said. He was on board and within 3 days we'd been approved to build a house.

When it was time for us to close on the house, we experienced delay after delay. Someone stole my husband's identity and opened up several accounts that began showing up on his credit report. By this time, my husband was in Afghanistan, and I was in the States living with my parents until we closed on the house. It was beyond stressful handling it all alone, but I persevered until one day a very rude customer service agent told me there was no way they'd remove the account from my husband's credit report, even with all of the evidence they had to prove it was fraudulent. I hung up the phone and broke down in tears. I'm not one to cry often from pressure, but that day I was incredibly frustrated. I can remember thinking it was the straw that broke the camel's back. I drove around crying and begging God to turn things around. I just wanted to close on our home and get the children settled before school started.

Through my frustrated mumbling, God whispered to my heart, "You'll close this month." This was the first day of July 2010. All throughout the month, various obstacles popped up, but I continued to come into agreement with God and repeatedly declared, "We will close on our home this month." Around the 3rd week of the month, God told me to call that company back. I was reluctant, but I trusted God, so I called again. This time a kind customer service rep answered the phone. I explained the situation and asked her to review the notes on the account. I told her how I'd sent all the documentation to prove fraud. I rambled until she cut me off.

"Call back tomorrow," she said.

I was confused. "Call back tomorrow?" I repeated.

I Am a Prayer Warrior

"Yes. This is a recorded line. Please call back tomorrow after 2pm."

Then it clicked. She was going to help me! I thanked her and ended the call. I followed her instructions and the following day we were cleared to close. We closed on Friday, July 30th at 3pm. It was the closing attorney's last closing on the last business day of the month, but it was God's perfect timing!

Prayer for Healing

In August 2015, my mother went into full pulmonary arrest. She was placed on a ventilator. She was running a high fever, retaining more than 100 pounds of fluid, her carbon dioxide level was dangerously high, and her oxygen level was dangerously low. My family and I took turns sitting with her in ICU, but she was totally sedated and too sick to be weaned from the meds. The doctors tried everything they could but had little hope of her recovering. They sat us down multiple times per week telling us she would either die or have severe brain damage, with little chance of living a normal life if she woke up.

The first week was an incredibly emotional time for me. I wasn't sure how to pray. I didn't want to be selfish and ask God to keep my mother alive if it was her time to go. I also didn't want her to leave prematurely. Since, I didn't know what God wanted, I just prayed for His will to be done, but I knew I needed to be more specific in my prayers. I needed to know God's will so I could come into agreement with it and decree it in the Earth.

There were 3 times per day that we were not allowed to be in the room with Mom. One of those times was from 12pm to 2pm. The very first Sunday of being at my mom's bedside, I took those two hours to go to church. I sat in the back of the same church I was called on to pray every Friday night as a teen/young adult. I knew that if I just got to the church, I'd be able to hear God clearly. I didn't want to talk to anyone. I didn't want special words of prayer. I just wanted to hear what God had to say about my mother and I knew if I could just get to the church, I'd be able to quiet my emotions enough to hear clearly.

By the time I got to the church, service was in full swing, so I slipped into the very last pew, a far cry from my normal position at the front of any church I visited. One of the members, the very woman I'd admired for her position as a prayer warrior, noticed me and came over to give me a hug. When she hugged me, I broke down into tears. She had no idea what she was going to get, but just her touch caused the flood gates to open. It was the warmth and kindness of her heart that allowed me to really weep. She prayed for me and allowed me to cry on her shoulders.

After I composed myself, we both took our seats and listened to the rest of the sermon. Now that I'd relieved myself of the emotions clouding my thought process, I was able to hear God clearly. As the Pastor preached, all I kept saying to God was, "Just tell me what the outcome is going

I Am a Prayer Warrior

to be. If I know Your will, I will be okay." Just as the Pastor finished the sermon, God answered me. "It's not over."

Armed with those three words, I exited the church and headed back to the hospital. I had a renewed energy because I'd heard from God. The medical team was still assembling us, attempting to prepare us for Mom's death, but I knew something they didn't know. God was going to save my mother's life. It wasn't over.

Over the next 2 weeks, I watched as my mother's heart rate plummeted multiple times. Each time, the nurses would start scrambling and yelling for the crash cart. I'd back up into the corner to give them space to do their jobs, but while doing so, I prayed. I commanded her heart to keep beating. When she developed a fever that would not break, I commanded her body's temperature to regulate. When the medical team told us about a risky procedure that could potentially save Mom's life, I gave them the greenlight to proceed, knowing all would be well.

While Mom was in surgery, I went on about my day as if nothing was happening. I knew the end. Therefore, I trusted God as I waited to hear the good news. Within 2 days of the procedure, Mom was awake. Seven days later, she was transferred out of the intensive care unit and into a long-term care facility. One month after that, she was transferred to an aggressive physical therapy clinic. Two weeks later, she WALKED out of the facility!

In the six years since my mother's illness, we've experienced several other medical emergencies, including a harrowing bout with COVID-19. Nevertheless, I've stood on the word the Lord spoke to me. My mother's story is not over. When she completes her assignment here in the Earth, she will be able to peacefully return to Heaven, but not a moment sooner.

As a prayer warrior, you must know God's will in every situation you take to Him in prayer. To BE a prayer warrior, you must be in alignment with His will. You must lay aside your emotions and what you want in exchange for what God wants. You must be willing to look opposition in the face and declare the word of the Lord! This is what it means to BE a prayer warrior. You are one who ensures the will of God is executed in the Earth through your prayers, agreement, and the legal decrees you release. Ask God what He wants, AGREE with Him, and then DECREE… demand the Earth and all of its inhabitants to come into alignment.

Affirmation

I am a profitable Kingdom Entrepreneur. God has already given me the power to be successful.

Scripture Reference

"Remember the Lord your God. He is the one who gives you power to be successful, in order to fulfill the covenant he confirmed to your ancestors with an oath."
Deuteronomy 8:18 (NLT)

Declaration

I decree and declare success is my portion. Everything in the Earth realm is coming into alignment to fulfill the promises of God for my life.

Chapter 5
I am a Profitable Kingdom Entrepreneur

Profitable- affording profits: yielding advantageous returns or results. (Merriam-Webster)

Kingdom Entrepreneur- One who operates in the realm in which God's will is fulfilled while organizing, managing, and assuming the risks of a business or enterprise.

To say I have always been interested in business would be an understatement. I've always loved the idea of being the one to call the shots. I wanted to be the boss, make the decisions, tell everyone else what to do, and make the most cash! I believe this stemmed from a saying my mother used to say to my brothers and me when we'd dare to question her decision making. She'd use her distinct Southern Mother attitude to loudly proclaim, "I pay the cost to be the boss." My young mind determined that in order to be the boss, I had to be the one to pay the cost. What my young mind could not fathom was the sheer weight and magnitude of that cost.

When I was in high school, we were required to do a senior exit project to graduate. This project consisted of a written paper, a product, and an oral presentation. Since it was a graduation requirement, the seniors were encouraged to work on this project all year long. Like most teenagers, I felt the project was ridiculous. My grades and test scores were impeccable. Why did I need a project to determine whether or not I could graduate? While this was an educational requirement, God helped me to see who I truly was long before I knew what was happening.

The only idea that came to mind while trying to come up with a topic was entrepreneurship. Of course, entrepreneurship is too broad of a topic, so I was encouraged to narrow the topic down. Being a minority woman who lives in the United States, I decided to focus on my own demographic. My final topic became, "Entrepreneurship Among Minority Women in the United States."

I researched the topic and wrote a top-notch paper about the obstacles women face in business, the glass ceiling, the rate at which minority women started businesses in the 90's, and success stories. For my product, I pretended to start an after-school program. Yes, you read that correctly. I told the presentation judges I'd run an after-school program for elementary aged students for 3 weeks. In truth, I used my experience working part-time at a daycare to create a fake record. I'm not proud of the lie now, but my 17-year-old mind thought it was brilliant.

Armed with my fake records, statistics, and charismatic presentation, I scored a nearly perfect score on my senior

I Am a Profitable Kingdom Entrepreneur

exit project. I was always a conscientious student, so the grade mattered to me, but what mattered to me the most was the information I gathered from my real research. My eyes were opened to the limitations and obstacles women must overcome in business. I learned how minority women faced backlash and harsh criticism, and how few banks were willing to loan them startup capital. Beyond that, I learned I could stand in front of a room and command attention while presenting my thoughts and ideas. I learned I could be funny and passionate, while delivering what others could potentially see as boring data. I learned how special it was to create something out of nothing. But perhaps the most important thing I learned was I not only wanted to be the boss, but I could also be really, *really* good at it.

From the time I graduated high school to date, I have owned and operated a commercial cleaning company, an in-home daycare, a multi-level marketing business, a publishing company, and a coaching company. I've worked as an independent contractor for the US Government, setting my own schedule and having the freedom to accept my choice of assignments. I've worked as a part-time Nanny. I've been a full-time author, and even a relationship coach. I've consistently and successfully contributed to my family's finances, whether I had a traditional job or not. I've tried my hand at things across many different industries and everything I've ever tried has seen a measure of success. My problem was, I didn't want a measure of success. I wanted the success God showed me in my dreams.

Otescia R. Johnson

In 2016, I self-published my first legal thriller. This was my sixth book, but it was my first time stepping into the legal thriller genre. I had no idea how to write a legal thriller. I didn't know any attorneys I could interview. I never sat in a courtroom to research the procedures. I just knew there was a story locked inside of me that needed to be told. Armed with my writing skills and imagination, I wrote the story I saw in my mind's eye. By May of 2016, the book became an Amazon bestselling legal thriller. It remained in the Amazon top 100 for six consecutive months. I didn't have a large following, a marketing plan, or even any real knowledge of how to make a book successful. Yet, there I was on a bestseller list alongside literary giants like John Grisham, Walter Mosley, and Scott Pratt.

Overwhelmed by the success of the book, I went to God in prayer. I thanked Him profusely as tears streamed down my face. He began to speak to me about my destiny. He reminded me of all the times He called me writer. Then He went on to teach me about the business side of publishing. Writing was a passion and a response to a divine call. God called me writer, so I learned to BE a writer. But at that stage of my life, He was calling me entrepreneur which meant I had to BE an entrepreneur.

During the next few years, God consistently taught me entrepreneurship principles from the Bible. Scriptures I'd read over and over again now began to come to life in a whole new way. I was gaining revelation in a way I'd never experienced. God reminded me of all the businesses He

I Am a Profitable Kingdom Entrepreneur

inspired, empowered, and enabled me to start. He reminded me that I've always enjoyed being the one to call the shots, but I'd shied away from the associated costs. I'd shied away from the late nights and early mornings. I'd shied away from the pressure to generate revenue. I'd flat out ran from the idea of hearing the word no. Like many people, I wanted the title of boss, but I wanted no parts of the costs.

In 2018, after listening to a friend of mine, Melissa Nixon, pray for entrepreneurs, I heard the Lord whisper to me, "Delete your resume." During her prayer, Melissa had mentioned getting rid of the possibility of returning to Corporate America. While I was already a full-time entrepreneur, I'd always remained mentally open to the idea of returning to work for the right employer. I'd applied for jobs with no response to my resume and application. I was studying the scriptures and learning more and more about my purpose as an entrepreneur, but I'd never closed the door to the possibility of traditional employment. I followed God's instructions and deleted my resume.

By March 2019, my business looked totally different. Not only did we have more clients than ever before, but I'd also replaced my previous full-time salary without including my book royalties. The business was sustaining itself, as well as our family financially. I was finally living in the revelation of what God showed me in the scriptures, because I'd finally learned to BE what I'd always been.

Walking in the truth of what God called me, led to me seeking His help to run the business. If a kingdom entrepreneur is someone who operates in the realm in which God's will is fulfilled while organizing, managing, and assuming the risks of a business or enterprise, I had to seek the will of God. Just like I'd sought His will as a prayer warrior, I needed to seek His will as an entrepreneur. All those years of learning how to BE a prayer warrior were also preparing me to BE a kingdom entrepreneur.

God made me in His image to fulfill His will not only when it came to praying for people and situations. He created me to fulfill His will in the boardroom, in banks, and in high-stakes business deals. God revealed I was a powerful atmosphere shifter, so I'd understand how my involvement with a project could literally shift the wind of favor in God's desired direction. He was cultivating a faith and belief system in me, so that I would readily pray and invite Him into business dealings. Each layer of my identity in Christ was laying the foundation for the next. All God required was for me to see myself as He saw me. He needed me to stop fighting and just BE me, the me He created me to BE.

As a profitable Kingdom Entrepreneur, I can now teach others how to walk in the fullness of this identity as well. I can use the profits God puts into my hands to travel and teach others how to walk in this layer of their identity. I can use my testimonies, experiences, and revelations of Biblical principles to inspire others to BE who God has called them to BE, so they too can see similar results.

As I have leaned into this truth of who God says I am, I have seen greater profits with less effort, more lives being

I Am a Profitable Kingdom Entrepreneur

transformed, more successful businesses being launched, and more Christians stepping into their true identity as Kingdom Entrepreneurs. I have witnessed the favor of God in contract negotiations, the hand of God opening doors previously closed, and families seeing the provision of God through their businesses. Witnessing God move in the lives of His children who have been crying out to Him in prayer has been the greatest reward of this agreement with who God says I am. This facet of my identity is much bigger than me.

As you embrace who God says you are, you'll also notice changes in those you are called to serve. Your life becomes a living modern-day example of what happens when someone comes into agreement with Heaven. Your experiences give others permission to believe what God has said about them. This allows you to serve others from a place of purity that glorifies the Father.

Now, I would do you a great disservice if I did not include some of the more challenging elements of being an entrepreneur. Yes, I have seen more money annually working as a Kingdom Entrepreneur than I ever made on any full-time job. Yes, I have watched and coached others to do the same. However, I have also seen low revenue months. There were many months in those early two years that made me question my decision to lean into entrepreneurship. It was in the lean times that God taught me to use the power that lies in my tongue and the dominion He has given me to issue the legal decrees that would change my financial situation.

One particularly difficult month, I became so fed up with money struggles that I just yelled, "Enough!" I wasn't quite sure who I was talking to, but I knew something had to change. I was driving down a dark road while this revelation was taking place, but I remained focused enough to continue driving. I wasn't crying or really even praying. I was simply opening my mouth without thought of what I was going to say.

> "I command the Earth to yield her increase. I command the winds of favor to blow in my direction. I command the wicked man to cough up my money and send it to me now. I am a faithful sower. I command the harvesting angels to go into the fields of Heaven and bring me my harvest now in Jesus' name."

I went on and on for what felt like hours but in reality, was only about ten minutes. This was one of the many times Psalms 81:10 (NLT) came alive for me. I was opening my mouth and Holy Spirit was filling it with good things. It was also a manifestation of Romans 8:26-27 (NLT).

> *"And the Holy Spirit helps us in our weakness. For example, we don't know what God wants us to pray for. But the Holy Spirit prays for us with groanings that cannot be expressed in words. And the Father who knows all hearts knows what the Spirit is saying, for the Spirit pleads for us believers in harmony with God's own will."* -**Romans 8:26-27(NLT)**

I Am a Profitable Kingdom Entrepreneur

Every time I've read this scripture, I assumed it meant Holy Spirit prayed for me only when I spoke in my Heavenly language or when I released groans. God has since given me a deeper revelation of this text. Holy Spirit prays for us every time we are weak and unsure of what to pray. The groanings mentioned in the text are only one example. There are also times when God needs us to hear the words Holy Spirit releases on our behalf so that we'll be armed with those prayers for future use. These are the moments Holy Spirit becomes a teacher. He equips us with the language we can then use to create legal decrees. Here's how I turned what Holy Spirit prayed through me into legal decrees.

- I decree and declare according to Psalms 67:6 (NKJV) that the Earth is yielding her increase on my behalf in Jesus' name.
- I decree and declare according to Ezekiel 37:9 (NLT) that the winds of favor are blowing in my direction now!
- I decree and declare according to Proverbs 13:22 (NKJV) that the wealth of the wicked is being transferred out of storage and into my hands in Jesus' name.
- I decree and declare according to Galatians 6:7-9 (NLT) that I am reaping the financial seeds I have sown. The harvesting angels are going into the fields of Heaven to reap my harvest and bring it to me now in the name of Jesus!

Armed with these decrees, I could now provide direction to the Earth realm, so that what was already established in Heaven could be manifested in the Earth. From that point forward, I began to release these decrees every time I felt God leading me to do so. I took dominion over my finances and commanded the Earth to obey. I learned to BE the profitable Kingdom Entrepreneur God created me to be before He formed me in my mother's womb. I learned to AGREE with what God has already established for me in Heaven. Then, by the power and unction of Holy Spirit, I learned to use the scriptures to guide me as I DECREE what God has already done. The result has been year over year increases in provision, favor, and revenue.

Affirmation

I am God's beloved daughter. He rescues me from the weight of the world and the heaviness of work.

Scripture Reference

"Now I will take the load from your shoulders; I will free your hands from their heavy tasks. You cried to me in trouble, and I saved you; I answered out of the thunder cloud and tested your faither when there was no water at Meribah." **-Psalms 81:6-7 (NLT)**

Declaration

I decree and declare my God has rescued me from the toil of heavy tasks. I rest safely and confidently in Him while all of Heaven and Earth are conspiring to bring what I need to me.

Chapter 6
I am God's Beloved Daughter

"Father to the fatherless, defender of widows- this is God, whose dwelling is holy. God places the lonely in families; he sets the prisoners free and gives them joy. But he makes the rebellious live in a sun-scorched land." **-Psalms 68:5-6 (NLT)**

My whole life I've heard the phrase, "God is a Father to the fatherless." I've referred to God as my Heavenly Father. I've listened as people have told their stories of how our loving Father God has healed them, provided for them, nurtured them, and more. I had a head knowledge of these things, but no heart revelation. It sounded good. I believed it to be true, but I had no clue what it meant to be a daughter. How could I really understand the depth of what it meant to have a Heavenly Father if I had no understanding of how to be a daughter?

When I wrote the first book in this series, I received so much healing and closure. The conversations I had with my mother and paternal grandmother provided answers to questions I never knew existed. I gained clarity on why I am so protective over my mother. I gained a deeper appreciation of the pain that led my dad to drink himself to death. As these women shared stories of things I said and did before my 5th birthday, memories that are so old, I can't seem to recall them, I learned a startling and painful truth. I'd never really been a daughter.

Sure, I had parents who did their best to guide me. Yet, I was always attempting to guide them. Apparently, at three years old, I slapped a beer from my dad's hand and yelled at him that he was going to hell for drinking. Also, around age three, I convinced my mother not to commit suicide. Again, I remember neither one of these instances, but according to my mother and grandmother, they happened.

I was always a child who felt she could figure it out. If my mother seemed to have a lot on her plate, I would not go to her for help. If I needed something, I just figured it out on my own. At eight years old I heard my mother scream in shock when she learned my dad died. She was crying hysterically, so I just went back to bed. I went to school the next day as if nothing happened. Then afterschool, when my maternal grandmother sat me down to let me know my dad passed away, I acted as if I was hearing the news for the first time.

At age eleven when I started my menstrual cycle, I kept it to myself for two days until I needed my mother to buy more sanitary products. For those first two days, I just used hers without saying a word. She didn't notice they were missing, and I saw no reason to tell her about it. When I

I Am God's Beloved Daughter

finally told her, I saw no need to tell her it was day three. I'd handled things. I did not need help.

I never felt like I didn't have parents. I never felt like an orphan. I loved my parents deeply and I knew they loved me. It just never occurred to me I was supposed to or even allowed to lean on other people. I was an action taker and problem solver. If I saw a problem, I fixed it. I was hardwired to solve problems as if I lived on autopilot… or so I believed.

I lived this way well into my 30's. It created many unbalanced relationships. People would come to me and share their struggles, and I would gladly offer any wisdom I had to share. Again, I wasn't doing this consciously. I was operating on autopilot. Someone had a problem; I had a solution. I cared about this individual, so I shared the solution. I just wanted to help. Yet, when I had an issue, I would not say anything to anyone. I never considered the possibility that people wanted to help me as much as I wanted to help them. The thought never even occurred to me. I wouldn't even ask God for help until I'd exhausted all my own solutions to no avail.

I eventually began to feel exhausted by my relationships. They felt very one-sided. One day God began to speak to me about becoming a better friend. He revealed my lack of vulnerability to me. People who cared about me wanted to help and support me, but I wasn't giving them the opportunities to do so. My friends weren't leaches. They didn't want to take anything away from me. They just wanted to do life with me. I slowly learned how to be a sister, how to share the ups as well as the downs. Yet, God wasn't done.

In 2016, I met Val Scarbrough. She was introduced to me as a client, but God had a much different plan. Over the next two years, I spent time with her working on a project we were both passionate about. In each encounter with her, I took something different away. I admired many things about her and enjoyed the way she embodied her personality and strength. Then, in 2018, God decided to introduce her to me in a brand-new light.

"This is your spiritual mother."

"What!?!? I don't believe in spiritual mothers God. Is that even Biblical?"

"Sit under her. Submit to her ministry and she will teach you how to walk into the next level."

I cried and cried and cried some more. I knew I'd heard God speaking to me, but I was terrified of being controlled. I was terrified of being hurt and mistreated. I'd seen too many people be spiritually abused by people they believed were their spiritual parents, and I wanted no part of it. Besides, I didn't want parents. Parents for me meant work. I've always had to parent my parents and make sure they were okay. Why would I need MORE parents? No thanks God. I'm cool on that. (That's slang for I do not want that.)

Although I was nervous, I chose to trust God. I shared what God said with my husband, and together we made the

I Am God's Beloved Daughter

decision to first join the church. From there, we agreed and recognized Pastors Eddie and Val Scarbrough as our spiritual parents. The only problem was I still didn't know how to be a daughter.

One day while speaking to Pastor Val, she asked me a question about a situation my husband and I were silently fighting. She asked why we didn't say anything. "I don't know. I never thought to ask for help. We're dealing with it. We're good." She very kindly but firmly stated, "That's pride."

Insert record scratch here… What? Pride? How is that pride? I wasn't intentionally not asking for help. I didn't need it. We saw a problem and we are fixing it. How is that prideful?

I didn't ask any of these questions aloud. Instead, like always, I allowed them to turn on the inside of me thinking I'd be able to come up with my own answer. After a few days, the statement still bugged me, so I went to God in prayer. "God am I prideful? Am I not asking for help because I am too proud?"

"Yes."

"Wait… what? How is that pride? If I realize I need help, I'm willing to ask. I didn't need help though. I can come to You for myself. It never even occurred to me to seek another person's help. You're my help, right?"

God remained silent as the questions and thoughts tumbled out of me. It took another two years before I gained the full understanding of what God was trying to teach me. When I met my mentor and brother in Christ, Pastor Clyde Lewis, and he led me through my identity coaching, one of the identities I received from Heaven was "God's beloved daughter." Pastor Clyde taught me how to sit with Holy Spirit to gain clarity regarding my true identity in Christ, and how my identity manifests in different circumstances and situations. I began a daily practice of sitting with Holy Spirit to gain a deeper revelation regarding each identity. When it was time for Holy Spirit to provide clarity concerning my identity as God's beloved daughter, He added the following confession.

"I am God's beloved daughter. I am well loved. I am well cared for. I am well provided for."

I wept as I heard these words. As if being played on a large jumbotron, my life began to flash before my eyes and clarity poured from Heaven. Our relationship with others is a direct reflection of our relationship with God. I could not accept my parents as true parents, because I never understood what it truly meant to have God as my Heavenly Father. I relied on my own understanding. I'd grown up, but I'd never been truly raised. I didn't allow anyone to guide me and share the wisdom I needed to avoid pain, strife, and heartache. In that moment, God wanted me to learn how to walk in the posture of a daughter, one who was well loved, well cared for, and well provided for.

I Am God's Beloved Daughter

My relationship with my spiritual parents immediately changed. Instead of feeling like I had to have all the answers, I began to ask questions and follow the wisdom that flowed from their mouths. God taught me how to be HIS daughter by giving me a human representation of His loving parental nature. They were not assigned to my life to hurt me, but to raise me in the ways of the Kingdom. I began to study the scriptures to find Biblical examples of spiritual parent/spiritual child relationships.

In each instance, I saw a leader in the faith, teaching someone else how to lead faith-filled lives. I studied the way Elisha respected Elijah and followed him, thereby receiving a double portion of the mantle that rested upon Elijah's life. I saw Timothy be elevated in ministry because of the teaching and training Paul shared with him. Timothy did not have to build from the ground up. He started from a place of elevation because he stood on the foundation Paul had already laid for him. Timothy did not have to question how to build a church, because Paul provided him with the framework.

Then God hit me with a double whammy. "Otescia, you were never fatherless. I've been here all along. I just needed to give you an Earthly example so you would recognize me." Cue the never-ending tears. I looked back over the toughest moments of my life, the times when I really didn't know up from down. In each of those moments, God guided me and showed me which way to go. When I needed to be comforted, Holy Spirit comforted me. When I needed insight or wisdom into a situation, Holy Spirit whispered guidance to my heart. When I felt all alone, Holy Spirit led me to a spiritual family who loved me.

Now, God was asking me to acknowledge and surrender to His position as my Father. He was asking me to BE His daughter, to release my need to figure things out on my own and come to Him first. He was asking me to put away my prideful way of thinking I could do this on my own. He was asking me to be vulnerable with Him as He leads me to all truth.

Some days, this submission comes through direct conversations with Holy Spirit. Other days, it comes through conversations with my spiritual mom as she talks to me on the phone, sharing her own life experiences with me. Every day, it manifests as a release of stress, anxiety, and worry. Before learning to BE God's beloved daughter, I lived in a constant state of stress. I was always worried about how things would be taken care of. The pressure was debilitating, but I'd done it for so long, I thought it was normal. Now, I know God never intended for me to live that way.

As God's daughter, I never have to worry about being provided for. He's not a deadbeat. He knows what I need and makes provision for me daily. (Philippians 4:19 NKJV) He would never give me a stone when I ask for bread. (Matthew 7:9-11 NLT) He loves me so much He literally sent His only son to the Earth to die for me. (John 3:16 NKJV). I am safe and secure. (Psalms 91 NKJV) I can trust

I Am God's Beloved Daughter

God to always lead me to His best (Psalms 23:2 NKJV) I don't need to have all the answers because I trust the one who knows what my future holds. If I ask Him, He will reveal these secrets to me, (Jeremiah 33:3 NLT)

My entire way of thinking and being changed when I gained revelation about my identity. God says I am His daughter. Just as I watch my husband protect and care for our daughters, God is watching over me, caring for and protecting me from dangers seen and unseen. It is His pleasure to bless me and give me the kingdom. (Luke 12:32 NKJV) This is why He sent Holy Spirit into the Earth to read the will and give me revelation of His infinite love towards me. Living from this truth has brought me into the greatest living revelation of God's love and provision towards me. I now live from a place of agreeance with Heaven which has given me permission to command the Earth realm to come into alignment.

Here are some declarations I release concerning my identity as God's Beloved Daughter. Feel free to add these to your arsenal and/or write your own to release daily.

Otescia R. Johnson

I am God's Beloved Daughter

I decree and declare I am well loved, well cared for, and well provided for.

I decree and declare the power of my tongue releases the will of my Father in the Earth realm. The way has already been made for me.

I decree and declare all of Heaven and Earth is moving to ensure my needs are met. I rest in confidence as God's will concerning me is executed.

I decree and declare my Heavenly Father causes me to rest in green pastures. Ease and grace are my portion in the Earth.

I decree and declare God has already given me everything I need for this day. I am complete. I want for nothing.

I decree and declare I shall see the hand of my Father at work in every area of my life on today. He assigned angels to watch over and protect me. I am confident in His protection.

Affirmation

I am a champion. I always win. No devil can defeat me. No trial can overtake me. Through me the knowledge of God is revealed in the Earth because I am God's mouthpiece.

Scriptural Reference

"But thanks be to God, who always leads us in triumph in Christ, and through us spreads and makes evident everywhere the sweet fragrance of the knowledge of Him."
– 2 Corinthians 2:14 (AMP)

Declaration

I decree and declare according to 2 Corinthians 2:14 (AMP) that victory belongs to me. God leads me into triumph in all situations, circumstances, battles, and trials. Every enemy that rises up against me is defeated in Jesus' name.

Chapter 7
I am a Champion

> *"But in that coming day no weapon turned against you will succeed. You will silence every voice raised up to accuse you. These benefits are enjoyed by the servants of the Lord; their vindication will come from me. I, the Lord, have spoken!"*
> **-Isaiah 54:17 (NLT)**

I remember the day I was first forced to fight back. I was around five or six years old. To say the children, I went to school with were less than nice would be an understatement. However, I was also a child with a wild imagination. I'd sometimes make things up. I had no idea I had the mind of a writer back then. I just liked to spice stories up. If there were two children teasing me, by the time I got home, there were four or five. If someone called me ugly, by the time I told my mother the story, they'd called me and all the dead people in my family ugly. Yes... I actually used that one once.

This particular day, I'd decided to run home as fast as I could to see how fast I could get there. The bus stop was a straight walk from my home, but it was a pretty good distance away. So, my mom couldn't see me until I was about a block or so from home. In the 80's it was common in our small town for elementary aged children to walk to and from the bus stop alone. Everyone knew everyone so none of the children were in any danger of being kidnapped. I wasn't running because I was afraid. I was running because I was full of unreleased creative energy.

When I arrived home, my maternal grandmother happened to be at our house. "Why are you running?" She asked me with concern all over her face.

Without even missing a beat or pausing to think, I blurted, "That girl was trying to fight me."

I have no idea where the lie came from. Sure, I was always teased, but no more than usual, and no one was trying to fight me. Yet, I bent over struggling to catch my breath while my grandmother yelled at me for running away from a fight. She taught me why it was important to stand up for myself. Then, she threatened me. I am purposely using her exact words as I remember them. I will not clean them up to make it sound pretty for this book.

> "I'll be here when you get home from school tomorrow and if you run home again, I'm gonna beat you, then I'm going to take you to that child's house and make you fight them again. You don't run from no fight."

Now, I know her words sound violent and unnecessary to some readers, but you must consider the timing of the incident as well as the environment of a small country town. Children regularly got into fist fights in those days. We'd

I Am a Champion

fight, then play together thirty minutes later like nothing happened. My grandmother, out of fear I'd become the town punching bag, was trying to teach me to defend myself. Going off of the lie I'd told her; she used her instincts to teach me how to fight back so others would not bully me. Instead, she taught her creative granddaughter how using words could alter any story and open the ending up to so many more possibilities. This has served me very well. Thanks Grandma.

From those days up until junior high school, I got into more fist fights than I can count. I was still an honor roll student, but I developed a reputation as a fighter. I was always short in stature and lacked the designer clothes and shoes everyone else wore, so I was an easy target for bullies. However, armed with a mouth that would speak on autopilot, I could hold my own in the trash talking department. This would always lead to some child's ego needing to attempt to shut me up. Since I knew I would not be punished at home for defending myself, I would use my words to incite others to hit me. Then once they did, I proceeded to do what I found to be fun… fight.

My 7th grade year, I got into so many fights, the administrators expelled me. Though I was an honor roll student, I still needed to take my end of year exams to be promoted to the 8th grade. The only reason I passed the 7th grade was because the principal allowed me to return to school to take my exams during teacher workdays at the end of the year.

Otescia R. Johnson

My 8th grade year, my family moved to a larger city. Previously, I'd known all of the kids at my schools. Their parents knew my parents. Their grandparents knew my grandparents. The whole town was like one big neighborhood where everyone knew everyone. Well, in the new school, I didn't know anyone, so I laid low. No one teased me at this school. No one really said much to me at all. I was ignored for the first half of 8th grade, so there were no fights. Eventually I made friends, agreed to be some new boy's girlfriend, tried out and made the cheerleading team, and began my old trick of running my mouth. By the 9th grade, I was nicknamed, "little Mike Tyson" by one of the administrators. My grades were still great, but my mother frequently received phone calls about my fighting.

If someone offended one of my friends, I was ready to fight. If someone said something I didn't like about me, I was ready to fight. If someone teased a complete stranger, I was ready to fight. It never took much for me to decide to use my fists. This continued well into my high school years when God began to teach me how to really fight. My fists were no longer needed, but my mouth would eventually win every single battle for me.

I Am a Champion

"For we do not wrestle against flesh and blood, but against principalities, against powers, against the rulers of the darkness of this age, against spiritual hosts of wickedness in heavenly places." **–Ephesians 6:12 (NKJV)**

I was around 16 or 17 years old when I heard this scripture being read in church. It was as if the gears in my mind were clicking in place as I listened. The lesson my grandmother taught me about standing up for myself was indeed necessary, I just needed to shift my method of fighting. God was going to use every part of my story for His glory. This meant all those years of fighting, the speed at which I was ready to go to war, and my ability to speak quickly without having to think of what I was going to say were all training for me to become the real champion God created me to be.

Throughout my adult life, I have submitted to Holy Spirit as He taught me how to walk in my identity as a champion. When faced with challenges presented through people, it can be easy to fall into old methods of fighting by yelling and using harsh words. However, I desire to draw people to God with kind words, not push them away by acting out of my fleshly nature. So, even when pushed to anger, I had to learn how to separate the person from the action. This allowed me to focus my attention on my true enemy, the devil. This has been a lifelong process, but when I acknowledge who my true adversary is, I can battle through prayer, confessions of faith, and declarations.

As I learned to truly BE a champion in the spirit, I noticed my Earthly triggers seemed to be less and less active.

Otescia R. Johnson

Instead of instantly boiling when someone said something hurtful, I let it go without it affecting my mood or countenance. Instead of responding harshly every time someone spoke harshly to me, I was able to remain silent or diffuse the situation. This happened because my mind made the shift. I don't need to yell at a human when it's the enemy who is motivating them to say what they are saying or do what they are doing. I know how to defeat Satan and it's not by yelling at another person or getting into a fist fight. I defeat the enemy by living in a way that brings glory to God and exercising my dominion in the Earth. I gained heart knowledge of 2 Corinthians 2:14 (AMP)

> *"But thanks be to God, who always leads us in triumph in Christ, and through us spreads and makes evident everywhere the sweet fragrance of the knowledge of Him."*

I am not trying to become a champion; I AM A CHAMPION because God always leads me in triumph! Even when it seems like the deck has been stacked against me, I will always come out on top if I follow God's lead. Even when the enemy paints a smoke screen to try to make me feel like I am losing, I can stand on the truth of God's word and BE a champion.

A champion sprinter does not look at a race and say, "I'm going to lose." No, a champion sprinter thinks like a champion, runs like a champion, and wins like a champion. Transitioning into your identity of a champion will require a similar mindset. You must know without a shadow of doubt that every situation ends with you on top. You must

I Am a Champion

focus your energy on dispatching your warrior angels to do battle for you so that the enemy will be defeated, and your victory will be released in the Earth realm.

Remember, the book of Daniel provides a perfect example of how angels will go to battle for humans. Daniel was able to see victory in the Earth because Michael was dispatched to do battle in the Heavenlies, so that Gabriel could be freed up to bring the answer to Daniel's prayer. When you are faced with a battle, you have the right to ask for Heaven to go to war with you. As a champion, I have a responsibility to release my voice in the Earth, so that what has already been established in Heaven will come to the Earth realm. Our victory has already been assured! We are not waiting for the outcome of the battle to declare victory. We are champions, so we ARE victorious.

As I learned to BE what God has already called me, I began to see victories in every area of my life. I've shared many testimonies with you throughout this book. Many of the battles I've experienced were life threatening or could have altered life as I knew it. Yet, I am a champion, which means, I came out of each battle without even smelling like smoke. This is what happens when you come into agreement with Heaven regarding your identity. Victory is sweatless because I am a champion, I agree with what God says about me and every situation I face, and I decree victory in every area of my life. I have mastered walking in agreement with God concerning the outcomes of the battles in my life. This agreement has given God permission to come into the

Earth realm and flex on my behalf. Remember, Heaven moves at the voice of God, but the Earth moves at the voice of God through man. You must use your voice to decree the outcome to see the manifestation of your victory.

You ARE a champion; speak like one!

Affirmation

I am a forerunner. I prepare the way for those who are coming after me. I am successfully completing this assignment through the leading of Holy Spirit.

Scriptural Reference

"Listen! It's the voice of someone shouting, "Clear the way through the wilderness for the Lord! Make a straight highway through the wasteland for our God! Fill in the valleys, and level the mountains and hills.
Straighten the curves, and smooth out the rough places. Then the glory of the Lord will be revealed, and all people will see it together. The Lord has spoken!" – **Isaiah 40:3-5 (NLT)**

Declaration

I decree and declare I am operating in the full weight, power, and authority of a forerunner. All of Heaven and Earth are backing me and the winds of favor and change are blowing in my direction in the name of Jesus!

Chapter 8
I am a Forerunner

Forerunner- a person or thing that precedes the coming or development of someone or something else; a sign or warning of something to come; an advance messenger. (Oxford Languages)

This is perhaps the most difficult chapter for me to write because it requires me to be very transparent regarding how I discovered this God-given identity. As a full-time entrepreneur and creative, I often learn lessons from a life experience that has pushed me to prayer. During those prayers, Holy Spirit brings revelation. One such experience happened while I was going through an emotionally difficult period. I could not pinpoint exactly why I was feeling so low. I wasn't depressed. My family was healthy. Business was progressing. Yet, I felt unfulfilled. Something was missing, and it was gnawing away at me.

While asking Holy Spirit to reveal what was going on, He spoke a very simple yet profound sentence to me.

"The emotional highs and lows creatives have to experience to feel inspired is what throws so many off course."

I knew it was significant, but I had no clue what it meant. I inquired further, and He continued to bring revelation to me.

"You are a forerunner. This means you will experience things that prepare the way for others. You will feel what they will feel in the future."

He then revealed a vision to me. I saw a vision of a person walking through a forest. With each step, the person was chopping down trees and clearing away debris. As they walked, they were creating a clear path that future travelers would be able to travel.

At the end of the vision, God spoke to me again. "This is you in the spirit. You are clearing a path for others to follow, just as John the Baptist cleared the way for Jesus."

Reader, if you've been paying attention while reading this book, you know this is where the record scratch goes. Did Holy Spirit just compare what I do to what John the Baptist did for Jesus? HOW? How is that possible? True to form, Holy Spirit continued to speak.

"Grab your notebook. These are the characteristics of a forerunner. Research these in the scripture and teach those who are called to be forerunners in their industry. The sadness you feel is what they are feeling. Help them understand what I am doing in and through them. They have asked me for help, and I am answering through you. Are you willing to allow me to do that?"

I Am a Forerunner

The list below compiles the characteristics of a forerunner, as shared with me by Holy Spirit. It was compiled by divine inspiration. I want to make it very clear this is what He shared with me personally and as such may not be recorded anywhere else. This is what has given me reservations about writing this chapter. As a scribe, it is imperative I am able to back up what I write with scripture. In this case, I was given characteristics, then directed to the scriptures to see these characteristics in the lives of those we study. With that said, I will supply you with the list, as well as some of the scriptures that provided the anchor I needed to understand my identity as a forerunner.

9 Characteristics of a Forerunner

- Often sees beyond their time
- Often feels isolated
- Often Attacked
- Can seem as though they are all over the place
- Often battles depression or depressive thoughts
- May not always be able to explain what they see
- Built Differently - Can handle things that would destroy others
- Lives a consecrated lifestyle
- Often lives a hidden lifestyle before anyone knows who they are

One of the most well-known forerunners of the Bible is John the Baptist. You can find his story in the first chapter of the book of Luke. Before John the Baptist was even conceived, an angel appeared to his father, Zacharias, and prophesied concerning the coming child. Not only did the angel reveal John's coming, but he also gave Zacharias specific instructions regarding what was permissible in the child's life, AND revealed John the Baptist would be filled with the Holy Spirit before birth.

Now, keep in mind, the Holy Spirit had not been released into the Earth realm when Elizabeth carried John. We know Holy Spirit was sent to the Earth after the death, burial, and resurrection of Jesus Christ. Yet, John the Baptist was such a forerunner that he was filled with the Holy Spirit while he was still in his mother's womb… before Mary even gave birth to Jesus. This is why John leapt in Elizabeth's womb when he encountered Jesus in Mary's womb. It was the Holy Spirit inside of the fetus that recognized Jesus.

From conception to his death, John the Baptist prepared the way for Jesus. He was the living example of a consecrated lifestyle, as well as a taste of what Jesus would be in the Earth. From being filled with the Holy Spirit from birth, to living a pure lifestyle, to performing baptisms… John the Baptist was the forerunner who laid the foundation for the work Jesus would do in the Earth. He was one of the greatest forerunners we can study in the scriptures, yet there was a forerunner who prepared the way for him.

If you read Isaiah 40:3-5 (NKJV), Isaiah prophesies about the life and assignment of John the Baptist. He was speaking roughly 700 years before John's birth, yet he was

I Am a Forerunner

using his authority in the Earth to set the stage for the one who was going to prepare the way for the Messiah. Isaiah was a forerunner to the forerunner. What he saw would not be accomplished in his lifetime, but he cleared the path. He established on Earth what had already been established in Heaven.

Another forerunner in the Bible is the woman described in Proverbs 31. It is my belief that she is an example, of a wife and mother who is simultaneously a homemaker and an entrepreneur. If you read the chapter, you'll see she is described as doing everything from cooking and sewing clothes to handling international commerce. Basically, she is the forerunner who seems like she is all over the place. There is very little cohesion to all the tasks she is described as performing, yet she was a forerunner for women in business, homemakers, mothers, and wives. Many women have gotten the courage to walk out their God-given destinies after reading about her accomplishments. She laid a valuable foundation that women are still building upon today. I am proud to say, while I too am a forerunner, I am also one of the women who is standing on her shoulders. She was a forerunner for forerunners!

Next, we can look at the life of Elijah. Out of all of the forerunners I studied, I most closely relate to Elijah because he battled assignment fatigue which led to depressive thoughts. In 1 Kings chapter 19, Elijah is notified of Jezebel's intent to kill him. Out of fear, he ran alone into the wilderness. While there, he prayed for the Lord to end his life. Now this may seem like an extreme prayer but allow me to really break down what was happening.

Elijah's life was dedicated to the service of the Lord. He was a prophet among prophets. He sought the Lord in all things and did exactly as instructed. Yet, instead of his commitment and yielded lifestyle bringing favor with man upon him, it brought the threat of death. The people he'd been interceding for turned their backs on God. They literally killed prophets and were trying to kill him too! (1 Kings 19:10 NKJV)

Have you ever done exactly what God said and expected a positive result, only to see the opposite? Can you remember how confused, sad, and/or hurt you felt? That's what led Elijah to pray for God to end his life. He was disappointed and tired of doing the work without seeing a change in the people he was assigned to help. This fatigue led him to spend more than 40 days in isolation. It was a deep dive into the aftermath of what felt like a failed assignment.

Reader, I have been there! I've done all the things. I've done all the work. I fasted, prayed, and believed. I wrote the vision. I made it plain. Yet, the outcome was similar to Elijah's. What I'd done in obedience to God simply did not yield positive results. It crushed me. The disappointment made me want to walk away from it all. I was tired of hoping for something, only to be let down. I was tired of feeling like I looked like a fool for believing. I understand Elijah's assignment fatigue because I lived and overcame it myself!

I Am a Forerunner

As I studied Elijah's life, I learned the depressive thoughts often come when you are in a time of transition. Elijah was in between the prayer for rain and meeting the one who would become his successor, Elisha. He was walking into the greatest reward he'd ever know (being raptured into Heaven), yet the enemy tried to make him throw in the towel.

This is the life of a forerunner. Sometimes the ones you are called to help will hurt you. Sometimes you will feel isolated and even a little crazy for believing for that which you have never seen. There will be moments it feels as though you are all over the place. There will be days you pray for God to just take the whole assignment away. Regardless of where I am in my forerunner journey, I now know my job is to simply BE.

God doesn't expect me to be a perfect forerunner. He expects me to just BE a forerunner. I was a forerunner when I cried out to God for relief. I was a forerunner when I felt isolated and alone. I was a forerunner when it felt like I was all over the place with all my businesses. I was a forerunner when it felt like no one was listening to a word I said. I was always a forerunner. All I needed to do was agree with this identity.

Once I understood and came into agreement with my identity as a forerunner, God taught me how to write declarations for this identity. When I release these declarations aloud, I am reminding myself and the entire Earth realm of what God has already established. They motivate me to remain focused and not get distracted by what I see. I want to end this book by sharing 21 of those declarations with you. If they resonate with you, feel free to release them over your own life.

Forerunner Declarations

I decree and declare according to Isaiah 55:11 (NKJV) that my words go forth and accomplish that which they are sent to do.

I decree and declare I am a forerunner among forerunners. I prepare the way for those coming after me.

I decree and declare the whole Earth is conspiring to draw my ideal clients to me.

I decree and declare I shall see God's hand at work in every area of my life and business.

I decree and declare goodness and mercy follows me all the days of my life. I do not fret about things present nor things to come.

I decree and declare Otescia Johnson is a household name that brings glory to God the Father.

I decree and declare I am never isolated or alone. I am surrounded by those who love and support me.

I decree and declare my business is successful because God has given me the power to be successful.

I decree and declare I shall lead those assigned to my life to the feet of Jesus.

I boldly declare the will of God will manifest in my life and everything I touch shall prosper.

I declare my mind is blessed and new creative ideas come feely to me as Holy Spirit guides my thoughts.

Otescia R. Johnson

I declare I live from a place of innovation. As a forerunner I am always at the forefront of new movements in my industry.

I declare my business is a beacon for those who need my services.

I declare the winds of financial overflow are blowing in my direction.

I decree and declare the works of my hands are blessed.

I decree my children and their children shall see the fruits of my labor and my entire posterity is blessed.

I decree the forerunner in me is mentally and spiritually strong. I am able to overcome any attack the enemy tries to throw my way.

I decree and declare the wealth of the sinner that has been laid up for me is being released into my hands daily.

I boldly decree I shall see the promises of God in the land of the living.

I decree and declare my recovery of all that has been stolen, withheld, or unjustly blocked by the enemy. Once the thief has been found out, he must repay times seven. I decree a seven-fold recovery in Jesus' name.

I decree the Earth is yielding her increase to me, and I am seeing the fruit of my lifestyle as a forerunner. All the seeds I've sown are returning a mighty harvest in Jesus' name!

Special Note from the Author

You have been given the keys to bring the days of Heaven into the Earth. However, keys are only useful when you use them. Do not let this be another book filled with tools and knowledge that simply collects dust on your bookshelf or wastes away in your eBook library. Instead, begin using what you have learned to radically transform life as you know it. Again, Heaven moves at the voice of God, but the Earth moves at the voice of God through man! Before you can see the manifestation of everything God has revealed to you in the Spirit, it must be released through the power that lies in your tongue.

> Be who God called you to be.
>
> Agree with what God has said about you.
>
> Decree a thing, and it shall come to pass!

Daily Affirmations for Forerunners and World Changers

I am fearless and free in my true identity. – 2 Corinthians 3:17 (NLT)

I am successful because God has given me the power to be successful. God has a covenant with me concerning my success. – Deuteronomy 8:18 (NLT)

I am safe and secure in the presence of God. He has given me the victory! – Isaiah 12:2 (NLT)

I am God's beloved daughter/son. He rescues me from the weight of the world and the heaviness of work. – Psalms 81:6-7 (NLT)

I am a skilled and effective speaker. When I open my mouth, God fills it with good things. – Psalms 81:10 (NLT)

I am new in Christ. The old me has passed away and a new me has emerged. – 2 Corinthians 5:17 (NKJV)

I am loved. – Galatians 2:20 (NLT)

I am privy to all God needs me to know. I have all the information I need to make sound decisions. – Jeremiah 33:3 (NLT)

I am in sync with God and ahead of the curve. I watch as He does new things all around me. I listen as He speaks the new thing to me. – Isaiah 43:19 (NLT)

I am victorious. God always causes me to triumph. – 2 Corinthians 2:14 (AMP)

I am an ambassador for Christ. God draws people to Himself through me. – 2 Corinthians 5:20 (NLT)

I am a giver. I give freely to the Kingdom out of the abundance of my love for God. – 2 Corinthians 8:1-14 (NLT)

I am a friend of Christ. He makes the plans of the Father known to me. – John 15:15 (NKJV)

I am chosen and appointed by Christ to bear fruit that remains. – John 15:16 (NKJV)

I am full of joy because I spend quality time in the presence of God. – Psalms 16:11 (NKJV)

I am strong because my strength comes from Christ. When I feel weak in my natural body, I take confidence that I am strong in Him. – 2 Corinthians 12:10 (NLT)

I am wonderfully complex. God was intentional as He crafted me in my mother's womb. He knows my inner most parts and made them to work exactly as He intended. – Psalms 139: 13-15 (NLT)

I am well provided for, and all my needs are met. – Philippians 4:19 (NLT)

I am forgiven and freed from the penalty of sin through the blood sacrifice of Jesus Christ. – Romans 3:21-26 (NLT)

I am a conduit for God's glory in the Earth. People see my good deeds and glorify God, the Father. – Matthew 5:13-16 (NLT)

I am complete in Christ. I lack nothing. – Colossians 2:10 (NLT)

I am more than a conqueror through Jesus. – Romans 8:37 (NKJV)

I am overflowing with blessings. – Psalms 23:5 (NLT)

I am walking in a season of great blessings and favor. Before I can catch my breath from receiving the last blessing, the next blessing is upon me. – Amos 9:13-15 (MSG)

I am confident in the daily provision of God because I seek Him first. As I seek God and His righteousness, He provides everything I need. – Matthew 6:25-33 (NLT)

I am successful and have everything I need to live a Godly life. – 2 Peter 1:3-4 (NLT)

I am healthy in body and strong in spirit. – 3 John 2 (NLT)

I am motivated by the pleasure of the Father. My work pleases Him and yields an eternal reward. – Colossians 3:23-24 (NLT)

I am equipped to complete every assignment God has given me. – Philippians 4:13 (NKJV)

I am consistently grateful and give thanks to God in all things. – 1 Thessalonians 5:16-18 (NKJV)

About the Author

Otescia R. Johnson is a skilled writer, ordained prophetess, captivating and innovative speaker, published author, and mentor. Born in a tiny town in South Carolina, Otescia has always dreamed of a life full of travel and philanthropy. As she grew older, she began to move towards business and entrepreneurship, two areas in which she excelled greatly. She studied Business Administration at Stevens-Henager College where she earned her Bachelor of Science degree. While she made a name for herself within her respective field of business, she found herself unfulfilled as her desire to help individuals overcome past difficulties began to consume her thoughts.

Otescia's desire to help people all over the world through her ministry materialized in January 2009, when she began to lead the Women of Virtue Ministry at the Grafenwoehr Christian Fellowship located in Grafenwoehr, Germany, under the leadership of Pastor James Fleming. In addition to the Women of Virtue, Otescia opened her home weekly and facilitated group sessions aimed at providing a safe place for women to be spiritually vulnerable.

In 2012, Otescia took her home-based sessions a step further and founded O. Johnson Ministries, an effort aimed at equipping the whole woman to walk in the fullness of her purpose! She then launched the "Healing the Hurt" conference, which speaks to the broken places women often try to hide. In addition to managing O. Johnson Ministries, Otescia is the founder of B.O.Y. (Bet on Yourself) Enterprises, Inc., a corporation that helps believers merge their faith and business as they navigate the world of entrepreneurship. She is also the bestselling author of 13 published books, as well as the creator of the *Magnetize Your Life* and *Roadmap to Publication* systems.

Otescia is a firm believer in the sanctity of marriage and enjoys being married to her best friend and biggest supporter, Lyndell Johnson. Lyndell and Otescia met in an unorthodox way that led them to live by the phrase, "God has a way of doing things so that it can't be mistaken as anyone else." They quickly fell in love and have devoted their lives to each other, their children, and grandchildren. They currently reside in North Carolina.

Connect with Otescia

To connect with Otescia, you may visit her website www.otesciajohnson.com to join her mailing list.

You may also follow her on social media:
Facebook: @AuthorORJohnson
Instagram: @o.r.johnson

To have Otescia speak at your next event, please direct your inquiry to: bookings@ojohnsonministries.com

www.ingramcontent.com/pod-product-compliance
Lightning Source LLC
Chambersburg PA
CBHW071457070526
44578CB00001B/376